God Theories

God Theories

Revised Edition

Ken Ungerecht

Library of Congress Control Number:		2010910865
ISBN:	Hardcover	978-1-4535-4417-4
	Softcover	978-1-4535-4416-7
	Ebook	978-1-4535-4418-1

This book was printed in the United States of America.

Rev. date: 05/07/2013

To order additional copies of this book, contact:
Xlibris Corporation
1-888-795-4274
www.Xlibris.com
Orders@Xlibris.com
82203

CONTENTS

Contents

One

Introduction

The question of whether there is a Supreme Intelligence that has influence in the universe and world in which we find ourselves is one that has intrigued, confounded, and plagued the minds of men as long as there have been minds of men. The answer to this question is one with profound implications. If there is a "God," does it mean we do have eternal life? Is there an unseen source of love and guidance that we can learn to draw upon to help us through a life that for many is a series of never-ending frustrations?

Like many people, and because of their profound implications, I believe the answers to these questions are worth pursuing. But the very pursuit has engendered much discord in the world. It is tearing us apart and our approach to it must change.

The consensus opinion is yes, there is a "God," but there is little beyond that. The primary reason is there have been hundreds of hypotheses put forth by various societies and individuals concerning the nature of any possible Greater Intelligence and these are often jealously guarded and extolled. We are told to believe this or believe that. "Just have faith" are the words from those supposedly in the know. This is true whether those "in the know" would label themselves Christians, Buddhists, Muslims, atheists, or you name the group.

The spiritual views most people embrace are a reflection of where they grew up. All major religions share the same essential belief set. They all profess conviction in a loving Supreme Being, eternal life, and a set of moral principles to live by. They have each acquired their own beautiful traditions. Most spiritual leaders advocate respect for the customs of other faiths. The main problem, however, is these customs frequently lead to rigid and emotionally held dogmas that are often in conflict with each other. When this leads to intolerance and violence, religion becomes more of a destructive force in society than a constructive force.

The principal reason for the detailed differences in spiritual convictions is that we are usually expected to maintain them on blind faith. Logic and reason are not commonly used to support religious views.

Today we live in a world where science and the rational seem to dominate how and what we think. Science is generally viewed as an antagonist to spiritual ideas. There is an increasingly loud segment from this community that would claim their discoveries have rendered the concept of God obsolete. I believe they are wrong and their own science will play an integral role in proving them wrong.

The application of logic and reason involves a cyclic and spiraling process that includes speculation, gathering evidence and formulating proofs. In this book, I have attempted to incorporate those activities in a unique way with the intent of helping to develop a greater understanding of who and what we are.

In a recent poll, the participants were asked whether they believed in the creationist, intelligent design, or the evolutionary theory of origin. That poll itself reflects a lack of what is needed if we are going to ensure an honest search for truth. There are many who would believe in aspects of all those theories. But in none would they find important ideas which reflect their overall personal views.

The primary purpose in writing this book was to stimulate a different approach to the questions surrounding our spiritual nature because it's clear the current one is not working well. It is intended to be efficient, readable, and informative. The hope is the reader will be encouraged to further investigation regarding the topics discussed.

Our world is in crisis. It needs solutions to problems and it needs them quickly. Violence, global warming, terrorism, over-population, and the methods we use to acquire and share resources are stressing our planet to its limits. I suspect we could all identify a more or less valid set of reasons why there is such turmoil. Most would agree somewhere in the mix is the negative impact from rigid and unyielding spiritual beliefs. This agreement, however, would come from several perspectives.

The atheists, for example, would say a fundamental reason for much of the strife in our world is due to a fear based, blind, and irrational belief in something that doesn't exist. But, as we will demonstrate in the following chapters, the atheists would also have us believe in an absurdity beyond all understanding of that word to join them in their cause.

But many passionately held beliefs by those who do profess sureness in a Divine presence are mutually exclusive and, therefore, cannot all be reflections of Truth. Some of these will ultimately need to be released.

God Theories strives to achieve a balanced approach in our search for spiritual understanding. It uses sound scientific principles to irrefutably show we are all inherently eternal and divine beings. Its primary aim is to prove a set of Principles of Truth that will enable us to establish a firmer base from which we can more coherently explore those elusive mysteries.

What happens to us when we die is, arguably, the most intriguing and important question we will ever consider. This issue is rationally discussed in a wonderful little book written by Marilou McIntryre entitled *Life is Forever—Get Used To It*. That label might seem a bit audacious, but it expresses both a conclusion and a sentiment with which I am in agreement.

Every person living today is both an heir and a steward of a magnificent world. We have a moral duty to leave this earth in at least as good a condition as it was when we came in to it. We are at risk of abdicating that responsibility. Following are three things we can do that would help to ensure those obligations are fulfilled.

1. We can come to know the Truth that we are going to live forever.
2. We can come to understand we are each solely responsible for the quality of every moment of that forever. In the everyday world of events, many of which seemingly come at us from we know not where, that idea often seems preposterous. It can't be true. But, when viewed from the greater perspective that we existed long before we came in to this world and will exist long after we leave it, we can begin to come to a greater realization of its truth.
3. Even though we alone must assume ultimate responsibility for the quality of our existence, we never have to work at achieving it alone. We can learn to cultivate friends and allies, both seen and unseen, who will be eager, able, and willing to help us make it what we want it to be. I am certain that array of co-creators and co-helpers extends all the way up to, and including, an Unfathomable Complexity we have come to call God, Goddess, All That Is, Jehovah, Allah, and various other labels. The name we give it is not important. That we can be essentially certain

such a Complexity exists, that it knows us, that it loves us unconditionally, and wants us to be happy, is, however, of great importance. Life is a gift. Ours is to learn to receive that gift and to learn to make it fun. Included in the package is the gift of choice. It is not required that we do, or guaranteed that we will, learn how to make life fun. But doing so is our ultimate reason for being. That purpose will not end when this physical life does. We will not take our physical achievements with us when we pass beyond this life, but we will carry with us what it is we have learned from that experience.

The most fundamental truth we can come to know is that we are eternal. In other words we will live forever. That is an idea that excites some people and frightens others. But whatever effect it has, if it is a truth, we don't have too many options. We need to either embrace it now or else begin to take the actions that will ultimately enable us to do that.

Experience they say is the best teacher. There is no doubt truth in that as well. But sometimes a rational understanding can be useful to help provide the impetus to begin the experience. Many people deny their spirituality because they see no evidence it is real. They have become mired in a life of frustration. From that we conclude such misery is not compatible with the existence of a God that loves us. But in such situations, it is not God who has turned from us, but rather we who have turned from God. We can change that direction whenever we choose, but occasionally we need a little nudge. The following chapters may provide that to some as it uses sound scientific principles to prove to a virtually absolute degree of certainty we do, in fact, live forever. Every moment of that forever is either spent drifting away from the Source of that existence or returning to it. The direction is always a choice. Logic and reason may not take us far into the unfathomable complexities of our spiritual aspect. But for some, it may serve as both a solid base and a springboard into the incredible journey of returning home.

Two

Science and God

We can say with confidence there will never be a double-blind experiment that has as its hypothesis either the statement "God exists" or "God does not exist". In other words, the concept of God will never be proven or disproven by a singular scientific experiment.

However, contrary to what many scientists might want to believe, scientific conclusions can be derived in ways other than from double-blind, repeatable experiments. They can arise through the systematic analysis of a series of experiments or events, whether repeatable or not. They can also result from valid mental and mathematical exercises.

No single one of these will ever prove or disprove the existence of "God", but any one of them could prove, or at least provide evidence for, the existence of spiritual or psychic phenomena that we might associate with the possible existence of "God". We may be able to use a set of them to extrapolate a conclusion one way or the other. There is a great deal of scientific evidence that can be applied to this effort. I personally believe an honest examination of this material overwhelmingly supports existence of that Intelligence we have come to refer to by that name.

Much of this originates from within the scientific disciplines themselves, particularly the field of quantum physics. We are just beginning to comprehend what this discipline has to offer in our efforts to achieve greater understanding of the universe in which we live.

Much solid thinking also comes from the intelligent designers. This group has been maligned by many sources as putting forth what they term a "pseudo-science". That label has been well-earned in many ways and I will not follow them to all the places their thinking takes them. But, at the same time, they have put together powerful arguments to support the central belief that a Greater Intelligence must be involved in how our universe was created and the way in which it functions.

Science has traditionally had a much broader meaning than it does today. In that historical sense, it simply referred to knowledge that can be logically and rationally explained and in the methods used to attain that knowledge. In the last 150 years, however, the word has gradually taken on a more restrictive meaning. Today many "scientists" seem to think the only place science can be applied is to a study of the physical attributes of our universe. In this book I assume the word's older and wider meaning is more accurate and that science can be applied to the study of any universal aspect.

The words truth and certainty are often used interchangeably. In ordinary conversation, it may be possible to do that without causing much damage. But, even here, we should be aware the words have different meanings and we need to have an accurate sense of their meaning when we use them.

Truth is an either/or condition that describes the state of a matter or idea. Truth either is or it is not.

Certainty, on the other hand, is a qualitative sense that comes in degrees about whether a condition is or is not Truth. There have been several words used to describe the degree of that sense.

Absolute certainty is knowledge that is fully understood, accurately relates every idea to every other idea, and is infinitely correct in every way. Under this definition it would be a given that absolute certainty is a state impossible to attain by human beings.

Virtual certainty is a state of conviction concerning the truth of a matter or an idea that is so thoroughly established by substantial support that a denial would be absurd. Humans clearly do have the capability to attain a state of virtual certainty. I am virtually certain, for example, the world revolves around the sun and not the other way around.

Most sound scientific conclusions come about in some variation of the following manner:

1. Establish the truth of a premise to a virtual degree of certainty.
2. Propose an idea about that premise that goes beyond the established truth.
3. Make additional valid assumptions related to the premise and the propositions.
4. Apply sound mathematical principles or repeatable exercises to the assumptions.
5. Use the mathematical or experimental results to arrive at a conclusion about the truth of the proposition to some degree of certainty.

One trap in this process is not ensuring the truth and validity of the initial premises and assumptions. If either of these are invalid, any conclusion that is reached will not be valid no matter how sound the mathematical application or how carefully the experiment is devised and performed. Unfortunately, this initial carelessness happens frequently in our efforts to establish truth and is a principal reason for many of our difficulties.

I will submit *God Theories* makes careful use of sound scientific principles to prove the following statements to a virtual degree of certainty that closely approaches an absolute degree.

1. None of us could have come into this world by chance, luck, or because we live in a universe that is compelled to produce something and simply wound up producing us.
2. Conscious involvement originating outside the physical realm had to be part of the process by which each of us did come in to this world.
3. The essence of who we are cannot possibly depend upon the creation of a particular physical body.
4. Therefore, the essence of who we are must exist both before and after any physical body in which it may currently find itself.
5. Therefore, we are all, in essence, eternal spiritual beings.

I will also state with a virtual degree of certainty these statements will, at some point, have to become generally accepted and important fundamental Principles of Truth. I do want to make it clear my book proves nothing more and nothing less than the statements listed above. A few people who read the earlier versions have made the claim it proves the existence of "God". I do believe in the existence of a Greater Intelligence that it is an integral part of how our universe functions. I do not, however, claim my book proves its existence.

If a spiritual aspect *is* an integral part of the human condition then it would also follow there *must* exist a set of truthful Principles that *does* accurately describe the characteristics and functionality of that aspect. The vastness and obvious complexity of such an aspect would virtually guarantee we will never be able to completely identify or understand *all* of these Principles. But, if we can *collectively* begin to identify and prove just a few of them, we will have laid a foundation upon which a true spiritual understanding can begin to be built that will profoundly transform the world.

Billions of things happen in our world every day and there are billions of reasons why they do. It is an inherent human drive to attempt to understand these causes. We cannot always do this, but sometimes we may be able to state important things about them even if we cannot identify specifically what they are.

The area of probabilities is an important discipline to which the rigors of mathematics are applied. One argument that often arises around this application is what determines when the probability of an event occurring by chance is zero. Some mathematicians have arbitrarily defined a probability of something that has less than one chance in 10^{50} of happening as, for all practical purposes, having zero chance of happening. In other words they would say the odds of 1/10000000000 000000000000000000000000000000000000 would be such a low probability it would have to be called a "mathematical impossibility".

I would agree with that definition and would add the opinion it is probably giving the benefit of doubt to possibility. These odds would be approximately the same as selecting one particular atom from all those making up our world. It is safe to say most scientific conclusions are arrived at with a far lesser degree of certainty than that.

Many people make extensive use of mathematics to help them formulate their beliefs. This would include proponents of both Darwinian evolution and intelligent design. Yet, even though both of these groups make wide-ranging use of mathematics, many of their conclusions are diametrically opposed to each other. How can this be? Well we could list many reasons, but I will simply say this; if we are going to live by the sword, we may have to die by the sword. In other words, if I use mathematical demonstrations to help establish the things I believe, and if a new mathematical demonstration shows an aspect of that belief set is wrong, then it would seem I have no reasonable choice but to do one of the following:

1. If possible, I can determine the new mathematical demonstration is in error.
2. I must modify my belief set so it comes into alignment with the new mathematical demonstration.

All too often what happens, instead, is an irrational argument that never goes anywhere except to a state of greater antagonism. There is truth in many arguments put forth by both the Darwinian evolutionists and the intelligent designers. But many are also mutually exclusive. Therefore, some must be wrong. The science used in *God Theories* discredits several passionate beliefs held by each of these factions. These will eventually either have to be adjusted or the science used in my book shown to be in error.

The most basic purpose of science is to use the tools of science to increase our understanding of how and why things happen in our universe and world. We are not able to tie together every cause with the effect it produces. But we do know every cause must be placed into one, and only one, of two mutually exclusive categories. These are by chance or not by chance.

If an effect occurs by chance, we say it was unplanned. In other words it happened without the intervention of conscious choice. If something happens not by chance, it means it was either fated to happen due to a sequence of mindless cause and effect events, or else it was planned through conscious choice.

We are not always able to fully describe a reason for why something happens. But, if we can scientifically identify which category a cause belongs in, that may lead us to important clues about that cause.

Many effects have more than one cause. We will now consider a situation that has both a by chance and a not by chance cause that involves conscious choice.

Let us assume a million people go out every week and buy a ticket. Let us further assume these tickets get thrown into a drawing machine. At the week's end a ticket is selected from the machine and one lucky person wins a million dollars.

In this situation the effect is somebody wins a million dollars. There are two easily identifiable causes producing this effect. One is the not by chance cause of buying a ticket. This is a conscious choice made by each of the million people. The other is the by chance cause of drawing the winning ticket. The effect of winning the million dollars requires both causes.

But let us now suppose the same person wins a lottery like this two weeks in a row. It would not be absurd to think this could happen. It is obviously not likely, but it could happen to somebody once every 25,000 years or so. You could even be that lucky person once every 15 billion years or so.

But let us now suppose the same person wins a lottery like this three weeks in a row. This, obviously, would be an extremely unlikely effect. Is it absurd to think it could happen? I would say yes. This would be something so unlikely I would consider it an absurdity to think it could happen by chance, and I suspect the law would as well. You can bet they would be mighty interested in taking a closer look at just what might be going on in a situation like this. They would be right in doing so, because now it would be almost certain we no longer have a not by chance and a by chance cause producing the effect of winning the million dollars. Now we would almost certainly have two not by chance causes producing this effect. One of these would be the conscious choice everybody makes of buying a ticket and the other would be the conscious choice someone is making with respect to the drawing machine. We may not know who is doing it or how, but we can be virtually certain somebody is doing something to manipulate the drawing.

Now, even though it is an occurrence that would not be expected to happen by chance more than once every 15 billion years or so, there are those who might argue it is not absurd to think somebody could win a lottery like this three weeks in a row. Okay, so then where is the point of absurdity? Is it four weeks in a row, five, ten, a hundred, a million, a billion . . . ? Eight weeks in a row would take us to the "mathematical impossibility" we arbitrarily defined earlier. I think, however, the idea that one person could win a lottery like this by chance three weeks in a row is absurd and the idea it could be done more than three weeks in a row is beyond any ordinary meaning we give to the word.

We will now expand on this idea and see how it applies to the first fundamental Principle of Truth we identified earlier in the chapter. That is that none of us could have come into this world by chance, luck, or because we live in a universe compelled to produce something and simply wound up producing us.

The process by which any of us do come into this world is, in many ways, much like the lottery example we have just discussed.

Two people, assuming they have the necessary qualifications, can make the conscious choice to have a baby. They cannot, however, consciously direct the particular sperm to the particular egg needed to begin creating the particular body to be used by that baby. In other words your parents may have made the conscious choice to have a baby nine months or so before you were born, but they did not make the conscious choice to have you. That happened because of a chance combination of a particular sperm and a particular egg.

Or did it? Might you have been born even if a different sperm/egg combination had resulted in creating a different body? We are so programmed by our society to believe we and our body are the same we have come to take for granted one cannot exist without the other. But the truth is that simply cannot be.

We will shortly show the mathematical possibility that any particular person, such as you or me, could ever be born into our world by the chance combination of a particular sperm and a particular egg is far less likely than the possibility one person could win a million dollar lottery even one billion weeks in a row. If the idea of winning such a lottery three weeks in a row is absurd, then the idea of winning one a few billion times in a row is so far beyond absurdity it could make one's head hurt to think about it. Therefore, the idea any of us could have possibly come into this world by chance is equally that far beyond absurdity. It is nonsense to suggest that is how it could have happened.

A mathematical proof used to establish a truth contains the following components:

1. Truthful premises
2. Valid propositions and assumptions
3. Correct mathematical manipulations applied to the assumptions
4. Resulting conclusions

What I would like to do now is lay out the proof we have been discussing in a more technical format by identifying each of its components.

The Premise:

The essence of each person currently exists in a physical form we call a human body.

The propositions:
1. This essence did not come into this body by chance or fate.
2. This essence cannot be dependent on the creation of a particular human body.

The assumptions:
1. The science of biology is correct when it states a human body begins its physical manifestation after the combination of a sperm from a man and an egg from a woman.
2. The science of biology is correct when it states a typical man produces approximately 1 trillion sperm in his lifetime.
3. The science of biology is correct when it states a typical woman produces approximately 400 eggs in her lifetime.
4. No one has ancestors common to both parents. (This assumption is not completely valid, but that will have negligible effect on establishing the resulting conclusions.)
5. The average time span between generations is 25 years.

For the purpose of this exercise, we will ignore the fact anyone's ancestors would all have to have met and gotten together in the first place in order for them to have any chance of ever being born.

If the typical man generates approximately one trillion sperm in his lifetime, and if the typical woman generates approximately four hundred eggs in her lifetime, and if our existence did depend on the creation of a particular physical body, that would mean the chance any of us had to ever be born is approximately 1 in 100 trillion or 1 divided by 100,000,000,000,000 or $1/10^{14}$. This last formulation is expressed as 1 divided by 10 raised to the 14th power or 1 divided by 10 multiplied by itself 14 times.

But each of our parents had to go through those same chances, as did their parents, as did their parents, as did . . . for any of us to have even this small chance. If we go back to the time before our grandparents were born to calculate our chances of being born, those odds become roughly 1 divided by 10^{98}.

How do we arrive at the number 10^{98}? To answer that question, we need to review some basic arithmetic. The rule applied here is, if we multiply two numbers with the same base number raised to some power, we simply add the powers. We have calculated the odds of any one person being born from two parents are about 1 divided by 10^{14}. We each have two parents and four grandparents who would have to have gone through the same chances. Therefore, if we go back to the point in time before our grandparents were born to calculate our odds of ever being born, we would have to multiply 10^{14} by itself seven times (once for us and one time for each of our two parents and four grandparents): $10^{14} \times 10^{14} \times 10^{14} \times 10^{14} \times 10^{14} \times 10^{14} \times 10^{14} \times 10^{14} = 10^{(14 + 14 + 14 + 14 + 14 + 14 + 14)} = 10^{98}$.

How big a number is 10^{98}? Well, let's just say it's big. It is also important to realize 10^{99} is a number even 10 times bigger, 10^{100} is a hundred times bigger, and so forth. To provide a more clear concept of the values of different powers of 10, I will list a few examples where =~ means "equals approximately to."

10^1 =~ the number of eggs in one dozen
10^2 =~ the number of miles between New York and Baltimore
10^3 =~ the number of miles between New York and St. Louis
10^4 =~ the number of miles half way around the world
10^8 =~ the number of miles to the sun
10^{21} =~ the number of atoms in a drop of water
10^{24} =~ the number of atoms in a glass of water
10^{50} =~ the number of atoms in the world
10^{81} =~ the number of atoms in the known universe
10^{82} =~ the number of atoms in ten of our universes
10^{98} =~ the number of atoms in 100 million billion of our universes

To put this into perspective, let us imagine we take all of the 10^{21} atoms in a drop of water and make each as big as a marble one centimeter in diameter and then lay them in a row. This would make a string of marble-size atoms that could stretch to the sun and back about thirty-three million times. The odds of picking one particular atom from this string would be roughly the same as winning the weekly drawing for the million-dollar lottery three straight weeks in a row.

But let us make the considerable leap now from the 10^{21} atoms in one drop of water to the 10^{98} atoms in one hundred million billion of our universes. Let us now pretend we make each of those atoms as big as a marble one centimeter in diameter and we lay them end to end. Let us further assume there is a being whose job is to walk along this string of marble-size atoms and, at some point, select one. Let us further assume, because of that selection, some lucky soul will come into existence and all other possible souls will not. Just for fun, let us pretend you are the lucky soul if this being selects atom number 69834597550021998723 76330911118567323998217643562234432873499822237746511213 13578993872237465263348 from this string of 10^{98} atoms and if any other selection is made, you will never exist. The odds of picking this particular atom would be nearly the same as winning the million-dollar lottery sixteen straight weeks in a row.

But it quickly becomes more ridiculous. If we go back twenty-five more years, to the time just before our great-grandparents were born, we have eight more people to consider in our calculations. Taking that into account reduces our odds to about 1 divided by 10^{210}. But no matter how far back in time we go, we can always go back farther, at least to the Big Bang. Therefore, the absolute value of yours or mine or anybody else's odds of ever being born based on chance alone extrapolate for all practical purposes to zero. I would submit, however, the odds reach absurdity long before the nonexistent point in time that would mathematically take it to exactly zero. Therefore, we can safely dismiss the possibility any of us got here by chance, which means we got here not by chance, which implies either fate or choice. But fate alone would give us the same impossible odds so we can dismiss that as well. Thus we must conclude conscious choice has to play some role of how and why any of us come into this world above and beyond the choice two people make to have a baby. This application of consciousness clearly does not take place within the physical realm. Therefore, it could only take place *outside* of that domain.

Even apart from this mathematical exercise, the evidence our universe is far more likely to be a product of intelligent mind than mindless happenings of natural forces is hard to deny. This evidence is equally persuasive that we are all, in essence, eternal spiritual beings currently experiencing a lifetime in what we call the physical domain.

The mathematical exercise I have submitted here is not the only one of its kind. There have been many who have calculated our universe could not possibly be what it is without a conscious intelligent force behind it. Lee Strobel's book, *The Case for a Creator*, is the best source for many of these I have read. In this book, Mr. Strobel intelligently discusses several mathematical exercises that suggest our world and our universe could not have become what they are today by the process of either random chance or evolution as it is generally conceived and taught to be. I do not dismiss the concept of evolution. That is a solid and well established science. But it does contain some long cherished aspects that are eventually going to have to be revised.

The mathematical exercise we have just discussed forces us to come to two important conclusions. The first is that conscious involvement from outside the physical realm had to be part of the process in determining how and why any of us came into this world. The second is the essential existence of any particular person cannot be dependent upon the creation of a particular physical body.

The mathematical calculations used to determine the odds of a particular person ever being born based on chance or fate alone are summarized in the table below back to a point in time only 3200 years ago. That is a long way from the 13.8 billion years since the Big Bang occurred. So the real odds, while they cannot be reliably calculated too much farther back, are far greater than any listed here.

The Mathematical Results

Years preceding date of birth	Number that, if divided into 1, will produce the odds of ever being born based on chance or fate alone
0.75	$1000000000000000 = 10^{14}$
25	$1000000000000000000000000000000000000000000 = 10^{42}$
50	10^{98}
75	10^{205}
100	10^{434}
200	10^{7154}
400	$10^{1800000}$
800	$10^{120000000000}$
1600	$10^{520000000000000000000}$
3200	$10^{10\,000000000000000000000000000000000000000}$

It was emphasized earlier how large a number 10^{98} is. We know it is roughly equal to the number of atoms in 100 million billion of our universes.

How big a number is $10^{1000000000000000000000000000000000000000000}$? It is incomprehensible. There are 1000 billion billion billion billion zeros in that number following the 1. If we were to write it out using Times New Roman font, size 12, single-spaced, it would require a sheet of paper 200 trillion miles high and 200 trillion miles wide. And, yet, if we divide that number into 1, the answer is the mathematical odds of any one particular person ever being born based on chance or fate alone beginning with a point in time only 3200 years ago and using the assumptions stated above obtained from the science of biology.

Now, I would not argue the chance of *somebody* being born into our world is low. Unless we do something that leads to our total destruction, it is clear the odds of somebody being born are extremely high. We have inherent built in forces at work to ensure that possibility is true. Rather, what I am talking about in the proof is the odds of a *particular* person being born into this world by chance or fate are low, in fact, absurdly low.

One could still argue even though the odds of a particular person being born by chance or fate are absurdly low, they are still never going to mathematically equal exactly 0, and that is true. One could also argue, along that vein, if somebody is going to be born it might as well be me as one of those other zillions and zillions and zillions . . . and zillions of possible people, and that is also true.

But if one is going to make that argument, he or she would also have to accept the argument that the odds for all the ingredients necessary to make a human being coming together by chance and then, "poof", combining with each other in exactly the right way to suddenly and spontaneously create a human being are also never going to mathematically equal exactly 0.

The truth is the possibility of any one *particular* person being born by chance alone and the possibility of a human being suddenly and spontaneously coming into existence by chance alone are "exactly" the same. That is, they are both essentially equal to zero. If we are going to believe in the possibility of one, then we must also believe in the possibility of the other, at least if we hope to maintain our integrity.

But even the world's foremost atheist, Richard Dawkins, does not believe in the "poof" theory of human creation. He knows to do this would be to believe in a ridiculous absurdity. But what he fails to realize, or at least to acknowledge, is that he is advocating an absurdity of equal magnitude in his "Blind Watchmaker" theory of undirected evolution. At some point, assuming he does want to maintain his credibility, he is going to have to either acknowledge a belief in spontaneous human creation or else modify his understanding of the evolutionary process.

I think it would make a lot more sense for him to consider how he might be able to modify his understanding of the theory of evolution. Along those lines, I would offer the opinion that the theory of evolution is ultimately going to have to expand its ideas to include, not only the evolution of forms as it currently does, but also the evolution of the consciousness's, souls, essences, whatever you want to call them, that inhabit those forms, but which exist in that essence separate from them. I do realize most evolutionists are going to go screaming and kicking into accepting that idea, but it is one in due course they will have to make.

The courts today are accepting DNA evidence as being proof far beyond any reasonable doubt. Convicted felons who have spent twenty years or more in jail are being released on that evidence alone. Others are being convicted using that evidence alone. Those things should be happening because DNA evidence does offer overwhelming proof of guilt or innocence.

Yet the typical odds produced by DNA evidence are "only" about a billion to one. One billion only has nine zero's after the one. That's not even enough to complete one inch of a line using Times New Roman font, size 12.

And, yet, there are those who would say a number containing enough zero's to cover a sheet of paper 200 trillion miles high and 200 trillion miles wide when divided into 1, does not provide proof beyond a reasonable doubt!!! That does seem more than just a little preposterous. The bottom line is we can only reasonably conclude none of us came into this world either by chance or by fate.

If none of us get here by chance or fate, that can only mean the process must require the use of intelligent choice. That choice must include more than the kind two human beings make when they decide to have a baby. It must also encompass conscious action occurring outside the physical realm. This application of consciousness would have to be involved in the process of planning how a physical body that is currently being created might be used by a being who is presently not in the physical realm, but who is preparing to enter that realm. We cannot reasonably doubt such conscious activity must be taking place. We do have room, however, for considerable speculation how such an application of consciousness is occurring and "who" is involved in doing it.

The second direct conclusion from the proof is that the existence of the essence of who we are cannot possibly depend upon the creation of a particular physical body. This conclusion would also imply that essence must both precede and succeed any body in which it is currently residing. This additional conclusion has enormous implications for both the theory of intelligent design and classical evolution. I would say the proponents for the classical theory of evolution have largely gotten it right. But, at some point, it becomes obvious we cannot reasonably be expected to continue thinking it is the mindless and chancy process most of those people would claim it to be. They have managed to convince the majority so far to accept that absurdity as truth. But the time will come when the consensus understanding will be that consciousness, from the tiniest speck to the most sophisticated gestalt, must exist both before and after any form in which, at the moment, it may find itself.

Three

The Anthropic Principle

A number of books have been written in recent years by several notable people that seem to have one overriding objective. That apparent purpose is to use the methods of science to demonstrate our universe did not need conscious intervention from outside the physical realm in order to evolve into what it has become. A composite of the thinking involved in that effort appears in Stephen Hawking's latest book, *The Grand Design*, coauthored with Leonard Mlodinow. This book posits our universe spontaneously and effectively created itself out of nothing. Nature's laws then took over and these have mindlessly and relentlessly led to its current state. There is no need in this theory to invoke the idea that any outside consciousness had anything to do with the process.

The authors do allow our universe is quite amazing even if it was self-created. They would also acknowledge there are aspects of it that seemingly do defy mathematical odds. An idea that has been put forth to try and explain away these seeming impossibilities is something called the anthropic principle. This concept was first coined by Brandon Carter in 1973 with the following statement. "What we can expect to observe must be restricted by the conditions necessary for our presence as observers." Clearly there is nothing controversial about this expression as it stands. In fact, it is quite obviously true. But several ideas have evolved from it that have proven more contentious.

One of these puts forth the notion there is no point worrying about the implication of the small probability of a particular effect happening if it has already happened and if that particular effect was part of a set of possible effects of which it was inevitable one of them would happen.

Now, again, there is no controversy around this statement as it stands. But the key word here is inevitable. Sometimes we may think something is inevitable when it is not. Most proponents of the idea that we live in a completely deterministic universe would say everything is fated or inevitable and there is no such thing as free will or conscious choice. In the mathematical exercise discussed in the previous chapter, however, we demonstrated that a belief in a fully fated or deterministic universe also requires a belief in an absurdity of unimaginable magnitude.

The people who promote the concept of a totally deterministic universe would like for me to use the anthropic principle and acknowledge, because of the simple fact of my existence, I must, indeed, be that "lucky" one. "Just think. From all the zillions and zillions and zillions and . . . . and zillions and zillions . . . . of possible people who could have been born from my long ancestral line, glory be and wouldn't you know it, it did just happen to be me".

I do find it interesting, however, that I have never seen Mr. Dawkins, or Mr. Hawking, or anybody else for that matter, actually use the anthropic principle to try to justify the impossible odds of their own individual and unique existence. I suspect that is because they either know to do so would effectively and immediately strip from it any validity it might possibly have or else they have never thought through just what those odds might actually be.

An analogy often used in an effort to validate this offshoot of the anthropic principle involves the examination of the chances of receiving a particular hand dealt from a deck of cards. If someone deals you a 13 card hand from a 52 card deck, the odds of you getting a hand are exactly 1/1 or, in other words, absolute. But the odds of getting any particular hand are exactly 1 divided by 635013559600 or approximately $1/10^{12}$. Now, those are indeed small odds. Yet, every hand that is dealt, simply by virtue of the fact that it was dealt, has beaten those odds. Hawking and Dawkins, and many other people as well, would say this is similar to how our universe works. They would agree the odds of you or me ever being born may be extremely small. But, since we know people do exist in our world, the odds of someone being born are, obviously, 1/1. The anthropic principle would then be used to say we just happen to be that lucky one and are, therefore, entitled to special assumptions regarding the laws of probability.

But we need to be careful about how we use an analogy to help us validate an idea because in one or more ways the analogy will be different from the idea. An analogy can be useful to help understand an idea, but it can never be used to validate one. From within the increased understanding, we may be able to find something that does help validate it. But there is no guarantee of that. We need to examine the differences between the analogy and the idea carefully to see if there is anything that may, in fact, refute our attempt to validate the very idea the analogy is helping us to understand.

One problem with using the deck of cards analogy to try to validate the concept of a universe that has no need of an outside or integrated consciousness is without the application of consciousness there would never have been a deck of cards in the first place. A universe is far more complex than a deck of cards. The ordinary laws of nature, fate, chance, and natural selection have all obviously played a role in helping make it what it is. But there is an enormous amount of evidence, even aside from the proof discussed in the previous chapter, to suggest a greater consciousness from beyond what we are normally able to perceive had to somehow be involved in the overall process as well.

The real difficulty, however, in trying to use this particular analogy to validate a completely deterministic universe has to do with the magnitude of the improbabilities we have been discussing. It is true enough that $1/10^{12}$ is an extraordinarily small chance of something happening. But it does not begin to compare to the odds any of us had of ever being born if we had to depend upon a mindless universe to do it. We have already calculated if we go back only 3200 years the odds of you or me being born instead of some other hypothetical person is roughly equal to $1/10^{10\,000000000000000000000000000000000000000}$. Those odds are about the same as being dealt the identical 13 card hand 400 billion billion billion billion billion billion billion times in a row.

One can only ponder the wealth that might be accrued from that sequential set of occurrences if the hand happened to be a 13 card straight flush. But there is not much point in doing that for long. It is a mathematical impossibility and so, therefore, are you. And you could beat and pound and squeeze and stretch and run the anthropic principle through the wringer 50 million times, but it is still not going to be able to bail you out of any attempt at either changing or denying that fact. You are not here by accident, you are here for reasons, you are an eternal piece of the Divine, and you do matter.

Nature is none other than God in things . . . Animals and plants are living effects of Nature; Whence all of God is in all things. . . . All things are in the Universe, and the universe is in all things: we in it, and it in us; in this way everything concurs in a perfect unity. . . . Before anything else the One must exist eternally; from his power derives everything that always is or will ever be.

(Giordano Bruno, 1585—DivineCosmos.com)

If we want to calculate the real odds any of us had of ever being born based on chance or fate alone, we cannot stop at 3200 years. We will have to go all the way back the estimated 13.8 billion years to the moment just before the explosion itself, or whatever it was that started the whole process rolling. The grand design theory put forth by Hawking and Mlodinow in their book speculates a universe springing forth from nothing. The theory further states the events that have happened since the release of that mysteriously created mass and energy follow a mechanical sequence of cause and effect. The logical conclusion from that idea means everything within that mysterious and original "stuff" would have to have been exactly right to initiate the particular chain of events leading to yours and my happy existence. One electron more, one proton less, one photon traveling in a slightly different direction, or any other slight alteration within that original primordial substance, whatever it consisted of, means a different sequence of events would have been started. In that case, it would not have been you and me pondering the mysteries of life.

The atoms making up a human being include roughly 4.7×10^{27} hydrogen atoms, 1.8×10^{27} oxygen atoms, 7.0×10^{26} carbon atoms, and a smattering from most of the other elements for an approximate total of 7×10^{27} atoms. If we took all those atoms, put them into a sealed container, shook it up real good, and let them settle out and begin combining on their own, I suppose there is an incalculable mathematical chance they would all come together to form a human being.

But even the Darwinians would say that is a ludicrous impossibility and could never happen. In fact, the theory of evolution was founded to provide logical explanations to discount ridiculous ideas such as that. But the classical evolutionists cannot have it both ways. They cannot say this idea is a mathematical impossibility and that one is not if the numbers are the same. Actually it would be far more likely that a human being could pop into existence by randomly mixing up the right atoms than it would be for you or me coming into existence within a completely deterministic universe. This is because there are far more pieces required to comprise a universe than there are to make a human. But that difference is beside the point. They are both mathematical impossibilities and, therefore, a fully fated universe cannot be the kind we're living in.

Stephen Hawking, Leonard Mlodinow, Lawrence Krauss, and Richard Dawkins are respected and visible people. They have each made significant contributions to our world for which we rightly feel gratitude. But too often we have a tendency to accept what people in their position say without fully examining what that is. We need to allow them to be as human and capable of making mistakes as the rest of us. The concept we live in a completely deterministic universe is enjoying a boom in popularity at the moment. But, as people begin to understand the magnitude of the absurdity they are being asked to believe in order to follow that philosophy, I do not think in the end it is going to have many takers.

I think our universe has sufficiently demonstrated it functions in a manner that will never require us to believe in absurdities as we attempt to more fully understand how it does operate. It surely contains great mysteries, including many we will likely never fully comprehend. It offers all manner of opportunity for human experience, including many we might rather do without. But we would be pretty hard-pressed to consider it a ridiculous invention. I am confident we can do better than resorting to utter incongruities in our efforts to more fully understand it.

The advocates of the classical theory of evolution would argue there are only two fundamental components that comprise our universe. These are matter and energy and consciousness is simply an eventual by-product of biological and chemical actions involving those two central constituents. But we have conclusively demonstrated consciousness is something that must also exist outside the physical realm. Therefore, consciousness must be another elemental component of our universe and it must be more than just a by-product of biological and chemical activity. It had to exist prior to the development of neural systems and it cannot be limited to the physical functioning of the brain. In the following chapters we will more fully explore those concepts in an effort to begin formulating more feasible suggestions concerning how our universe really does work.

Before proceeding, however, I would like to take a moment to make sure we unambiguously understand the difference between a proof and a speculation. I have received criticism in the past for expressing ideas without providing adequate evidence to support them. In every case I thought that was for ones I had made sufficiently clear were speculations. I want to ensure that criticism does not happen again by making a sharp distinction between what I consider to be proofs and what I consider to be speculations regarding the concepts discussed in this book.

By definition, a proof is something consisting of a body of knowledge and for which there is enough evidence to establish the truth or falsity of a concept to a high degree of certainty. A speculation, on the other hand, is just that. It is an idea put forth that may or may not have evidence or reason to support it. Speculations often flow out of proofs. A speculation may become a proof, but, in general, there will not be sufficient evidence to currently claim it as such.

I will contend the five conclusions reached in Chapter one have all been scientifically established as fundamental Principles of Truth. In other words the ideas that none of us could have come into this world by chance or fate, that conscious involvement from outside the physical realm had to have played a role in how we did come into this world, that the essence of who we are cannot possibly depend upon the creation of a particular physical body, that the essence of who we are must both precede and succeed any physical body in which it may currently find itself, and that we are all in essence eternal spiritual beings, have all been established to this point in the book as being true to the high degree of certainty I would consider necessary to be considered proofs.

I will further maintain the only way the conclusions listed above could not be considered proven is to acknowledge a belief instead in an absurdity of unimaginable proportions. I would also be inclined to ask anyone who would deem them not to be proofs to define exactly what they think is required to attain that degree of certainty. I would further expect them to coherently explain why they believe the evidence we have examined does not contain those requirements. For my part I intend to continue with the assumption they have been sufficiently demonstrated confirmations of Truth.

Beyond that I will say much of the remainder of the book will consist of what I would call speculations flowing from these proofs and these will be supported by different levels of reason and evidence. I do have strong beliefs regarding many of them and would claim reasons for doing so. I want to make it plain, however, it is not my intent to assert any of them reach the degree of certainty I would feel necessary to be considered a proof.

Four

Matter

Matter is defined as that which occupies space and has mass. This definition is, however, neither complete nor totally accurate as we will see.

There are three fundamental particles of matter. These are the electron, the proton, and the neutron. These come together to form atoms. There are ninety-two different kinds of atoms found in nature. Atoms are different because they contain different numbers of protons, neutrons, and electrons. Hydrogen is the simplest element. Most hydrogen atoms contain one proton and one electron and no neutrons. Uranium is the most complex element appearing in nature. All atoms of this element contain ninety-two protons and ninety-two electrons with a varying number of neutrons.

Atoms come together following well-understood laws to form larger particles called molecules. There are literally billions of different kinds of molecules. Molecules vary in complexity from a single atom to several million atoms. Large groups of molecules are responsible for what we, as human beings, can detect with our senses of sight, sound, smell, taste, and touch. There are also many we cannot detect with any of these senses.

Besides the basic particles of matter, there are around 150 subatomic particles that have been discovered. Many of these have been given fancy names such as quarks, fermions, and leptons. Some of these are basic building blocks of protons, neutrons, and electrons. Others are short-lived particles created in experimental circumstances.

One group of subatomic particles make up what are called the bosons. These are important for several reasons. First, they do not have all the characteristics we normally associate with matter. Some have no mass, for example. Others have the capacity where more than one can occupy the same space. Bosons exhibit characteristics of both matter and energy. One of the most well-known from this group is the photon which is the basic unit of energy present in electromagnetic fields. Another is the graviton which is believed responsible for carrying the force of gravity. Gluons are the carriers used to hold together the protons and neutrons in the nuclei of atoms. There is much that has been learned about these subatomic particles, but there is also a great deal not yet known and many of their characteristics will likely remain a mystery for a long-time.

The basic unit of mass is the gram. 454 grams weigh one pound on earth. An important unit of mass used at the atomic level is called the atomic mass unit. This is the amount of mass present in one proton and is 1,836 times the amount found in one electron.

In addition to all the particles that have been identified, hypothesized, and characterized by scientific means, many people, both from within the realms of traditional science and other disciplines, have postulated the existence of thought particles. It is impossible at this time to verify their existence by current scientific methods, but there is data to support it. In addition, it is not illogical to suppose their existence. I deem it likely science will eventually acquire the means to verify a basic unit of consciousness as being something that is a part of all matter and energy. There is an increasing amount being written about this topic, although much of that is conjecture. However, postulating the idea of thought particles and units of consciousness could fuel powerful logic that may help us come up with potential answers to some of the daunting questions that have swirled around the human condition since its inception—whatever it was that brought it about.

If an aspect of consciousness is part of every particle of matter, it is easy to imagine it as being capable of providing an instinctive guiding force in uniting these particles into ever-increasing complexities. Postulating the concept that consciousness units are an inherent part of all matter and energy may allow us to begin to fill a few of the "gaps" left by the theory of evolution in its attempt to explain the methodology used in the creation of these complexities.

Some of the greatest names in the history of science, particularly those working in the field of quantum physics, have expressed a belief in the existence of consciousness at the most basic levels of matter and energy. These include such notables as Max Plank, Niels Bohr, Alfred Lotka, David Bohm, and others.

Plank is often considered the father of quantum physics because he was the first to observe that energy existed in discrete states. From this observation, he determined what today is referred to as Plank's constant. This value is used to determine the energy content of a waveform as a function of its frequency. The idea that Plank retained a belief that consciousness is something inherent in all matter is frequently supported by the following quote:

"I regard consciousness as fundamental. I regard matter as derivative from consciousness. We cannot get behind consciousness. Everything that we talk about, everything that we regard as existing, postulates consciousness."[1]

The evolution from classical Newtonian physics to quantum physics produced a paradigm shift in the way many people view the universe. Classical physics deals with the macroscopic. At this level events can be predicted with virtually absolute certainty. We have what is often called the "billiard ball" effect where one event leads inexorably to another. For example, if I hold a rock in my hand and I then release my grip, we can be pretty sure it will fall to the ground. We have observed these kinds of events happening over and over again and have defined a number of what are called "universal laws" to describe and categorize them.

But at the quantum or subatomic level, many of these laws no longer hold true. We cannot predict with any degree of certainty the exact behavior of any one of these particles. In many instances, they either seem to have a mind of their own, or they are affected by the thoughts of the observer. It is possible to predict with a certain degree of probability some of them will do this and others will do that, but we cannot say absolutely this one will do that and that one will do this. This behavior is summarized in Heisenberg's principle of uncertainty. This principle says that "by precise inequalities that certain pairs of physical properties, like position and momentum, cannot simultaneously be known to arbitrary precision. That is, the more precisely one property is measured, the less precisely the other can be measured. In other words, the more you know the position of a particle, the less you can know about its velocity, and the more you know about the velocity of a particle, the less you can know about its instantaneous position.

According to Heisenberg its meaning is that it is impossible to *determine* simultaneously both the position and velocity of an electron or any other particle with any great degree of accuracy or certainty. Moreover, his principle is not a statement about the limitations of a researcher's ability to measure particular quantities of a system, but it is a statement about *the nature of the system itself* as described by the equations of quantum mechanics." [2]

There is still debate, even among quantum physicists, as to the scientific and philosophical implications of this principle, but it does leave open a multitude of unanswered possibilities concerning our understanding of the nature of reality.

Five

Energy

Energy is defined as that which is either at the moment giving motion to matter or at some point in the future has the potential to give motion to matter. These two states of energy are classified as kinetic and potential.

The classic example used to illustrate the two states of energy is that of a rock sitting on the edge of a cliff. As long as the rock continues to sit there we say it has potential energy with respect to the bottom of the cliff. If a force comes along and pushes it over, we say it has kinetic energy of motion as it falls to the bottom. During its fall the potential energy it had while sitting on top of the cliff is being converted to kinetic energy providing it motion as it falls to the bottom. Kinetic energy is a function of an object's mass and its velocity. During the time it is falling the velocity of the rock will be constantly increasing and, therefore, so will its kinetic energy. Just before it hits the bottom the potential energy it had while sitting on top will all have been converted to kinetic energy and it will have reached a maximum velocity. When it does hit the bottom all this kinetic energy will be transferred to whatever it hits. Perhaps what it hits will also be set in motion. Maybe sparks of electrical energy will be generated. But eventually the rock and everything it hits will stop moving due to opposing forces such as friction. The rock will have lost the potential energy it had while sitting on top of the cliff and also the kinetic energy it possessed while falling to the bottom. Ultimately, all this energy will take on the form of heat which will randomly dissipate into the surrounding environment.

This simple example illustrates several basic characteristics of energy. First, we have seen energy can exist in two primary states, potential and kinetic. Second, we have illustrated energy can exist in several different forms. For example, the potential energy existing in the rock while it was sitting at the top of the cliff did so in the form of gravity. The energy in the rock while it was falling existed in the form of mechanical and its state was kinetic. Some of the energy transferred to objects at the bottom also existed in the form of mechanical and was kinetic. Some may have been converted to the form of electrical as electrostatic sparks or to light as electromagnetic waves. When the transfer is to the individual particles of matter, such as atoms or molecules, we no longer call it mechanical. Instead we call it heat. This is a form of kinetic energy which gives motion to these smaller particles. Heat is considered the lowest form of energy. The natural tendency for all energy is to "fall" into this lowest state.

Another illustration would be that of a car moving down the highway. While it is moving, we say the car has mechanical kinetic energy. This existed initially as potential energy in the chemical bonds holding together the atoms in the gasoline molecules. These bonds are broken when the molecules combine with oxygen. This process converts the gasoline into water, carbon gases, and energy existing in the form of heat. The heat forces the gases to slam into the car's complex mechanical design which gives rise to its motion. Some of the energy also gets converted into heat which is dissipated into the road. If the car is going up a hill, it takes on potential energy in the form of gravity. This energy may be recovered for future use, but that which is converted into heating the road cannot, at least not as far as this particular trip is concerned.

To summarize, energy exists at any given moment in one of two primary states—potential or kinetic. Energy exists at any given moment in one of several forms. These include, but are not limited to, the following:

- Gravity
- Mechanical
- Electromagnetic or light
- Electrostatic
- Chemical
- Nuclear
- Sound
- Elastic
- Heat

Consciousness is a great mystery. It has been studied by classical science, but these studies have almost always been at a gestalt level. These studies have assumed consciousness exists exclusively in conjunction with some kind of neural system. These are legitimate experiments and we have learned a great deal from them. However, those studies cannot assume consciousness is not a fundamental property of universal substance able to exist apart from neural systems. And simply because it has not been "officially" studied or been classified as a fundamental property by classical science, does not mean many people, including many from the scientific community, have not thought about it in those terms.

One interesting particle that has been hypothesized by classical quantum physicists, and which many believe they have finally isolated, is from the boson family. This unit is called the Higgs particle after one of the scientists who predicted its existence. It is believed further study of the Higgs boson will help yield greater understanding as to how other particles which have mass attain that mass.

There has been a tremendous monetary investment in the effort to isolate and identify this particle. Its possible discovery was announced on July 4, 2012 as a result of decade's long work at the European research agency CERN in Geneva, Switzerland. More investigation is needed to establish this to a reasonable degree of certainty. But it is going to be interesting to see where further exploration of the Higgs boson takes us with regard to a greater overall understanding of the functionality of our universe.

Six

Laws of Thermodynamics

The first law of thermodynamics says energy can be neither created nor destroyed. Under most ordinary circumstances this statement is, for all practical purposes, true. In our example of the car we learned how the chemical energy in the gasoline molecules was converted into mechanical energy and heat. If the lights and radio were on other forms of energy would also be produced. In this example the total amount of energy lost from the chemical bonds in the gasoline molecules was almost exactly equal to the total amount gained in these other forms.

However, at the quantum level the distinction between matter and energy is sometimes hard to determine. Einstein's famous equation, $E = mc^2$, predicted an equality between matter and energy. This was dramatically demonstrated to be true over the desert of New Mexico in 1945. What this exercise showed is that matter and energy are two different forms of the same thing. This meant the first law of thermodynamics had to be slightly altered to say the total amount of matter and energy in the universe remains constant and under extraordinary circumstances one can be converted into the other. I think you could get any person from Japan to agree this seemingly slight adjustment to the first law of thermodynamics can have great practical, and sometimes devastating, significance.

This adjustment to the first law of thermodynamics also has profound implications strictly from both scientific and philosophical perspectives. What we are saying here is both matter and energy spring from the same fundamental substance. This fact raises many interesting questions for which we are all seeking greater understanding. What is this basic substance that brings forth both matter and energy into our universe? Why and how does some of it become matter, and why and how does some become energy? Why does some which becomes matter do so in the form of an electron, some a proton, some a neutron? Why does some which becomes energy do so in the form of light or gravity or the binding force of neutrons? What role does the Higgs boson play in all of this? What is the role of thought and consciousness at this most basic level? We may never know the ultimate answers to these mysteries, but we do know enough to expand our contemplations about their ramifications.

The second law of thermodynamics states the entropy of an isolated system which is not in equilibrium will tend to increase over time. In other words, particles of matter governed by physical laws as we have observed and defined them, tend to become randomized, disordered, and chaotic if they are not given some sort of direction. The reason matter tends toward an entropic state is because, without an external force such as gravity or choice acting upon it, the tiny little pieces making it up have an equal probability of going one way as another. Gravity, wind, instinct, and choice, among other things, are able to create order out of disorder by selectively applying directed force to these pieces of matter when there otherwise would be none. Thus, we have things in our world such as the Grand Canyon, bird nests, toothpicks, Cadillac Seville's, and Boeing 747s.

If the predominant theory attempting to explain the origin of the universe is correct, the greatest order and, therefore, the least amount of entropy we can imagine, existed just prior to the Big Bang. The only thing we can envision today capable of producing such order is some application of consciousness. It is for this reason at least a few modern-day astronomers believe some level of it must have been involved in generating this concentration of universal substance.

Seven

Consciousness

What exactly is this thing we call consciousness? Does it exist only in conjunction with neural systems, or is it something able to exist independently? Does it require neural systems to transfer information from one part of a living organism to another? Or, does it use this capability as but one way of expressing and making use of its very beingness? Is it found only in living organisms? Is there a minute level of it that exists within every particle of matter or unit of energy? If there is, is the consciousness of an atom greater than that of an electron? What about the consciousness of two chemically combined atoms? What really is a gestalt of consciousness? Can consciousness exist completely apart from matter as we know it? Is there a near-infinite level of it existing within the mind of a Supreme Being whose ultimate characteristics we cannot even begin to imagine?

Consciousness is a word we don't have a good definition of, but we do have a sense of its attributes. Following is a list containing several of these along with two or three basic definitions. Definitions can often only hint at the full meaning of any word. I might suggest as you read through this list you take a few moments to ponder the following questions. Could some level of this characteristic be an attribute of the consciousness of an atom, a tree, a human, or a being capable of setting into motion the events that have led to the current state of our world and universe?

Instinct
1. A powerful motivation or impulse
2. An innate capability or aptitude

Awareness
1. Having knowledge of
2. State of elementary or undifferentiated consciousness

Cognition
1. The mental process of knowing, including awareness, perception, reasoning, and judgment

Knowing
1. To perceive directly
2. To grasp in the mind with clarity or certainty
3. To regard as true beyond doubt
4. To discern the character or nature of

Reason
1. The capacity for logical, rational, and analytic thought; intelligence
2. To persuade or dissuade (someone) with reasons

Conscious
1. Having an awareness of one's environment and one's own existence
2. Subjectively known or felt

Intuition
1. The act or faculty of knowing or sensing without the use of rational processes
2. Instinctive knowledge or belief

Imagination
1. The formation of a mental image of something that is neither perceived as real nor present to the senses
2. The ability to confront and deal with reality by using the creative power of the mind; resourcefulness

Desire
1. A wish or longing
2. To express a wish or make a request for; ask for

Understanding
1. Characterized by or having comprehension, good sense, or discernment
2. The ability to learn, judge, make decisions

Wisdom
1. The ability to discern or judge what is true, right, or lasting; insight
2. The ability or result of an ability to think and act utilizing knowledge, experience, understanding, common sense, and insight

Memory
1. The mental faculty of retaining and recalling past experience
2. The capacity of a material, such as plastic or metal, to return to a previous shape after deformation

Love
1. An intense emotional attachment
2. A deep, tender, ineffable feeling of affection and solicitude toward a person, such as that arising from kinship, recognition of attractive qualities, or a sense of underlying oneness

Consciousness is defined in the dictionary as "the quality or state of being aware of an external object or something within oneself". That isn't much, but it is probably the best we can do for the moment.

In the concept of a completely deterministic universe everything that happens is established by what has happened before it. The people who believe in such a universe would say if we knew the precise conditions of everything at a given instant in time we could predict with absolute certainty the conditions of the next instant in time.

Some of these thinkers, such as Daniel Dennet, would suggest that does not, however, mean there is no such thing as free will. If I understand Mr. Dennet correctly, he is saying the process of evolution over time enables the creation of a synergistic condition making it possible for the robotic like actions of individual brain functions to create an overall state of free will. That is an over simplification of what he is saying, but I believe is the heart of his argument. It is an interesting one and contains merit, but it will require a few adjustments. The brain is the primary source of consciousness while we are physical and is a rather important part of our ability to function successfully during the time we spend here. But it cannot be the only basis for this phenomenon.

The process of sequential cause and effect is one method by which many things do happen in our universe. The observation of this fact has reinforced the generally accepted conclusion from classical Darwinian evolution that consciousness is something that has somehow come into being in conjunction with the development of neural systems in animals.

This conclusion from classical evolution has also been bolstered by recent advances in our understanding of the brain. We know we can stimulate certain areas in the brain and induce predictable conscious results. This observation has led many to conclude consciousness is "simply" the result of chemical and biological activities. Many notables in the fields of evolution and neural science have extended this idea to conclude this is the only way consciousness can be produced. They are, of course, unable to produce any science to support that rather bold extrapolation of this kind of brain experiment.

If we do use science and its methods to formulate at least some of our beliefs, and if a new sound application of science and its methods conclusively proves a portion of an originally established belief is wrong, then we have the two options I mentioned earlier. We can either seek to demonstrate the new application is in error or we must seek to modify our belief. I have confidence the science we applied earlier in the book is valid. Therefore, the commonly accepted ideas regarding how consciousness came into our world and how it is generated are going to have to be revised.

Even so, Stephen Hawking, Richard Dawkins, and others of their common philosophical bent are brilliant people who have contributed much to the understanding of our universe. One of the thoughts Mr. Hawking has put forth I find particularly fascinating is that universes may bubble up from nothing and there are many such creations. He also suggests each of these nascent materializations will move forward from that original point of formation and mindlessly evolve in whatever way it is fated to do. This would likely be in accordance with natural laws that somehow become uniquely balanced of their own accord within that evolving universe. This balance would bring forth a set of conditions that would likely be different from those of the universe in which we happen to find our own being.

Any thinking along these lines, no matter who is making it, would be primarily conjecture. However, I do think he may be on to something here. But since I do not believe in mathematical impossibilities, or absurdities of any kind for that matter, modifications will be required for what I understand Mr. Hawking's views on this idea to be.

I feel it unlikely such universes would spring from nothing. They may, however, spring from something with many of the same properties as nothing. These properties may be similar to the Higgs boson as it exists in its purest or precursor state. This "something" would likely have a net content of zero mass, zero energy, and zero consciousness. That would give such a "something" the appearance of nothing. Those would also be the properties of what many eminent thinkers have termed the universal substance, primordial essence, or basic ether. Any of those terms are adequate to label what would have to be the most basic of all "something". We could not call such a "something" matter or energy or consciousness, but it would be "something" containing the potential to be transformed into any of those.

The concept of the primordial ether has been bandied around the physical and metaphysical sciences for a long time. Not surprisingly, it has generated controversy in the process. Most proponents of string theory would likely not suggest it is what their science is studying. But what they describe sounds interestingly similar to a variety of the scientific and esoteric descriptions that have been made through the ages about this theoretical and mysterious substance. We will have more to say about that comparison later.

The idea there might be many universes is one gaining momentum in the scientific community. Some scientists postulate the existence of an infinite or near infinite number of universes existing in a space outside of our own. Others suggest there are parallel universes existing within the same space as our own. A few, such as Mr. Hawking, who believe in completely deterministic universes, suggest if there are enough of them it is reasonable to assume at least a few would evolve in in the finely tuned manner ours has. That theory may help to explain how a universe could evolve in such a way as to sustain life in general. But it still could not account for the unique existence of any particular consciousness within that domain. To do that for a particular universe such as ours, we would have to postulate an infinite number that are *almost* exactly like it. If we did that, we could as easily postulate there are an infinite number that *are* exactly like it. That would also mean there would be an infinite number of you and an infinite number of me and an infinite number of anybody else who has ever lived. If that is the reality, we are obviously not simultaneously aware of all those other individual selves. I'm sure we would be quite crazy if we were. That would also mean we would simply repeat the life we are currently experiencing for all eternity over and over again. As might be expected, there is no evidence to support that theory and I have serious doubts about its validity.

I do believe, however, there is legitimacy in the general concept of multiple universes. It is another example of an idea long held in metaphysical thought that physical science is just beginning to seriously consider. None of us, though, are in a position to understand it on an intellectual level to any significant degree.

Most consideration in recent years involving the questions of our spiritual nature, or lack thereof, has been dominated by two main groups. These are the Darwinian evolutionists and the intelligent designers. The "dialogue" that has taken place between these groups has literally included a series of highly publicized debates at the end of which each side has routinely proclaimed "victory".

In these "discourses", both groups have brought forth powerful arguments to support their own point of view. They have also managed to point out significant flaws in the other side. These deliberations have not been without value, but they are missing key ingredients if we are ever going to resolve the questions that keep dangling after each altercation. In the following chapters we will examine the dissonance that has come from these exchanges and see if we can filter out a few nuggets of truth.

Eight

Theories of Origin

There are several theories which have been put forth regarding the origin of our universe, our world, and mankind's place within it. I think most people would claim a belief in varying degrees to one or more of these theories. I suspect truthful elements can be found in all of them. In this chapter, an elementary examination of what I perceive to be the major ingredients of the two most commonly discussed ones will be provided. A third will then be considered which fills some holes present in each of the other two.

1. Classical Evolution

The principle component of this theory is the idea that the universe came into existence with what has come to be called the Big Bang 13.8 billion years ago. The best estimate for the age of our world is 4.5 billion years. That began with a gradual accumulation of gases which slowly condensed into solid and liquid form. Ever-increasing complex inorganic molecules began to form through chemical attractions and other natural forces. Molecules containing carbon subsequently began to develop with ever-greater intricacy. In time, the molecules which we associate with life began to form. Over eons of time and through a great series of random events (mutations), adaptations, and "natural selections", these molecules have evolved into the complex life forms we know today along with many others which have since become extinct.

It should be pointed out most classical evolutionists realize these events are not truly "random." They recognize a "direction" to them but would ordinarily not subscribe this to any level of consciousness but rather to the "forces of nature." The quantum physicists, however, are beginning to show us ever more distinctly we don't know as much about those forces as we perhaps once thought we did.

The classical theory of evolution does not assume the necessity of a greater intelligence than is known about today by classical science as having played a role in the overall process. This does not mean all proponents of this theory would deny the possible existence of such intelligence. This theory is also the one used to describe the origin and development of life as it is taught in most high school and college biology classes.

Most concepts associated with the classical theory of evolution are well established and have been demonstrated to be scientifically sound. However, we have demonstrated two of them to be logical absurdities. These are the ideas that consciousness is something that could have arisen in conjunction with neural systems in animals and that consciousness is strictly a function of chemical and biological activity in the brains of animals.

2. Intelligent Design

The core of this theory is an assertion there are certain universal features best explained by an intelligent cause, not an "undirected" process such as natural selection. Although most proponents of this theory are Christians, advocates of many of its precepts are not limited to adherents of this religion.

The consensus opinion among the scientific community is that it is a pseudoscience because it presupposes the existence of a divine, eternal, perfect, unchanging, and all-knowing creator. This, they say, is not testable by their methods. The main objections put forth by those who criticize the intelligent design theory center around the perplexity of who designed the designer.

This is a legitimate question and is probably one we will never be able to fully answer. But that does not provide justification for substituting a belief in one absurdity for the perceived idea if we don't do that we are forced to believe in another. That makes no sense at all. It is neither more nor less likely "God" came into being by chance or fate than you or I did. They are equally absurd ideas. But that doesn't mean such a Being couldn't exist any more or any less than it means you or I couldn't exist. We didn't get here by chance or fate either, but we are here.

I think part of the problem is our perception of what the characteristics and qualities such a designer would have. I do think such a complexity would be divine and eternal. But I doubt it would be perfect, unchanging, or all-knowing. I also do not believe such a complexity would be separate from its creation. But, regardless of what the exact qualities might be, there have been many mathematical formulations besides the ones put forth in this book that overwhelmingly indicate our universe could not possibly be what it is without some form of consciously directed intervention. The exact characteristics of the being or beings from which that consciousness came, and whether its source was from inside or outside the sphere of our existence, are completely separate questions from the problem of trying to determine whether or not such a complexity exists. They are, however, usually the ones at the heart of the "discussions" between the Darwinians and the intelligent designers. That is likely the main reason there doesn't ever seem to be much headway made from these deliberations.

The term "intelligent design" came into use after the Supreme Court ruled in 1987 against a Louisiana law that required the teaching of "creation science" whenever the classical theory of evolution was also being taught. Although the term "intelligent design" has primarily been put forth by proponents of the "Christian God," as a result of this ruling, the idea there must be an underlying intelligent force behind the creation of the universe and world in which we live is not a new one. Various forms of it have been put forth by many thinkers for a long time.

> *God and the world of Nature must be one, and all the life of the world must be contained within the being of God. . . . it is improbable that the material substance which is the origin of all things was created by divine Providence. It has and has always had a force and nature of its own.*
>
> *(Cicero—DivineCosmos.com)*

The structure of the currently most visible form of the intelligent design theory appears to be built around three main ideas. These are a fundamental belief in the Bible, a set of mathematical exercises used to demonstrate the nature of our universe requires the involvement of a greater intelligence beyond our current ability to comprehend, and some thought provoking questions about whether classical evolution is able to adequately describe how at least a few of nature's life forms have come to be.

It appears most intelligent designers completely discount the theory of evolution except for it being a factor in influencing changes in certain characteristics of members within a species. Their "official" position seems to be that different species of life have not evolved from a common source, but instead were created separately. Many of the questions this group has with regards to evolution are legitimate and without easy answers. In my view they do provide additional evidence some kind of instinctive direction has to be involved in the overall evolutionary process. But, to go from serious and intelligent questioning of evolution's basic principles, to a complete rejection of the entire theory is taking them quite a ways out on a rather shaky limb.

The greatest weakness I see in the arguments put forth by the intelligent designers, however, is their insistence on trying to apply legitimate science as a means of supporting the traditional views of one religion. Aside from their reasonable use of mathematics, most of their ideas are sourced in the teaching of the Bible. Specifically they appear to embrace the idea people must accept Jesus Christ as their personal savior if they hope to have a happy existence after their current physical one.

I find much to admire in the Christian religion. It is my heritage and I love tradition. Christmas is a magnificent time of year. Many of the literal and metamorphic teachings from the Bible that are ascribed to Jesus contain great wisdom and we would be well advised to pay them greater heed. I believe Jesus was a spiritually evolved being who lived in this world and who, in a mysterious way, is available as a friend and source of strength at times we might need those. I also appreciate the passion associated with members of this faith, at least up to the point where it leads to blind adherence at the cost of reason.

"I do not feel obliged to believe that the same God who has endowed us with sense, reason, and intellect has intended us to forgo their use."

(Galileo Galilei, DivineCosmos.com)

Great truths can be found in every religion. But each has also produced ideas completely incompatible with each other. Therefore, they cannot all possibly be true. Painful though it may be, the time has come for a more open and honest effort at trying to figure out which of those we are going to have let go. The literal idea that a loving God would condemn those He loves to a state of eternal torment simply because they cannot come to believe an irrational idea has got to be one of those.

The fundamental Christian precept that Jesus died on the cross to provide a means for us to get to heaven is even being challenged from within the evangelical movement. This is evidenced by the book *Love Wins* by Rob Bell. Mr. Bell has received much criticism from his peers, but his book contains coherent thinking from an important source vital in this discussion. It is one that took courage to write and Mr. Bell deserves significant credit for having done so.

3. Instinctively Directed to Consciously Driven Evolution

This theory is one that does not get a lot of publicity, but aspects of its basic principles have been around for a long time. They have been expounded in one form or another by such thinkers as Plato and Aristotle. In 45 BC, Cicero proclaimed the "divine power is to be found in a principle of reason which pervades the whole of nature." It is the kernel of much metaphysical thought and the overall concept is certainly not mine. But the following is my current interpretation of this philosophy.

1. There is an eternal and formless basic substance making up our universe which some people call the universal ether.
2. This ether holds all of the potential necessary to give rise to expressions of consciousness, energy, and matter as we know it and in ways we cannot begin to imagine.
3. Elemental units of consciousness are the most basic expression of this ether.
4. These consciousness units in conjunction with the various conditions of matter and energy, both known and unknown, become associated with each other in many ways we do understand and in many more ways we do not.
5. The consciousness aspect, operating at an "instinctive" level, provides a drive in even the most elemental forms of matter to take from its environment that which it needs to reproduce and add to itself. In other words, it provides an additional directing

force to the evolutionary process besides those we would ordinarily attribute to the "forces of nature".

6. Thus, some level of consciousness exists in and around every atomic and molecular structure, including, but not limited to, those we would traditionally call "living" or organic.

7. "Survival of the fittest" succeeds up to a point in creating ever greater and more efficient complexities of matter and consciousness.

8. However, if the complexity becomes too efficient in taking from its environment that which it needs to sustain and reproduce itself, or if the environment changes in ways the complexity is unable to adapt to, it is in danger of becoming extinct.

9. At some point in the evolutionary process, complexities we would traditionally call "living" began to form.

10. Today we have an incredible array of these "living" complexities.

11. At least one of these complexities, the human being, has evolved its consciousness to the level we would call "being conscious", or to the point where it has become "aware of itself."

12. The development of the attribute of "being conscious" is a major point in the evolutionary process for many reasons. Most importantly is the fact that freedom of choice becomes available. Gestalts of consciousness can begin to choose to behave in ways that will either enable them to adapt and increase their complexity in unimaginable ways, or else exhaust their environment and thus face the danger of extinction.

As one can see, this theory has many ideas similar to that of classical evolution. The primary difference is that consciousness is considered to be a fundamental participant in the entire process. This is a significant distinction and it allows us to easily imagine a seamless gradation of "consciousness's" ranging from the very least to the very greatest.

A brief and incomplete summary of the three theories is outlined in the following table.

	Classical Evolution	Intelligent Design	Instinctive to Consciously Driven Evolution
Eternal Essence	"Mindless" matter and energy	Divine, perfect, unchanging, omnipotent, and all-knowing God	Universal substance with "unlimited potential" of conscious expression
Major Source	Scientific theories and knowledge of biology, chemistry, and physics, and theoretical extensions	Bible and mathematical examples demonstrating infinite or near-infinite improbabilities	Scientific theories and knowledge of biology, chemistry, and physics, and theoretical extensions
Major Evidence	Scientific hypotheses, resulting experiments, and logical extrapolation and interpolation of the data	Mathematical examples demonstrating that much of the life existing in the world today could not have arisen without an intelligent guidance. These examples have generally been extrapolated to the teachings of the Bible.	Scientific hypotheses, resulting experiments, logical extrapolation and interpolation of the data, and anecdotal evidence of unexplained phenomena coming from religious and metaphysical sources

Nine

Speculation Evidence

The number of people who would subscribe to a belief in a totally deterministic universe does seem to be on the rise. Most would claim their conviction is based on science and they are simply going where that science leads them. But that conclusion is based instead on a scientific absurdity. It is constructed far more on emotion than it is on reason. It is not "testable by any scientific means" and it requires an inference from the evidence that is without substance.

There are many things that do happen in our world in a deterministic cause and effect manner. But to take that obvious truth to the ultimate deduction that everything is predetermined is not only without the validation suggesting that is something we should do, but, as we have seen, there exists much to suggest it is something we should not do. The science we have already brought forth in this book should be enough by itself to stop us from performing that extrapolation, but there is extensive additional material suggesting caution against the rashness of such a move. Before we continue I would like to take a moment and review several crucial facts we have established to this point.

1. The anthropic principle is an obviously true statement. It can be legitimately modified to help us understand many things including mathematical impossibilities. But it cannot be used to suggest, let alone prove, the possibility of an impossibility no matter how often or how vociferously the effort to do so is made. That statement, it would seem to me, is as obviously true as the principle itself.

2. The universe in which we live cannot possibly be totally deterministic.

3. Consciousness is not something that could have come into being in conjunction with the development of neural systems as classical evolution suggests it does.

4. Consciousness is not something that can be produced *only* as a result of chemical and biological activity in brain cells as many neuro scientists suggest it does.

5. None of us could have come into this world by either chance or fate. Therefore conscious choice had to be part of the process by which we did come into this world. Some of that conscious involvement had to be occurring outside the physical realm.

6. The essence of who we are cannot possibly be dependent upon the creation of a particular physical body. Therefore, the essence of who we are must both precede and succeed any physical body in which it may find itself at any given moment. Therefore, the essence of who we are is eternal.

If consciousness could not possibly have come into being in conjunction with the development of neural systems, when and how did it come into being? Was it with the plants or the minerals or is it something inherent in everything? If conscious involvement outside the physical realm is part of the process of how we come into this world, to whom does that consciousness belong? Does at least a portion belong to us? Are we at least partially involved in planning our excursions into the physical? If so, for what reason? Is this something we will do forever, a never ending merry go round of struggle in an unfriendly world? Will we move beyond that process to more fulfilling and exciting adventures? If so, is this a choice we can make? Is there a source of unfathomable knowing and love available to help us make that choice? If that is true why is there so much misery in the world? Does the analogy of radio station bands more accurately describe our universe than the deck of cards analogy does? Do we tune into transitory experiences at different vibratory rates in a way somewhat analogous to how we tune into radio stations? What did Jesus mean when he talked about "Many Mansions" in John 14:2? Is some method of reincarnation a primary feature of how our world functions? Can reincarnation help to explain the seeming inequities in our world? Is it really accurate to say life begins at conception? Would it be more accurate to say the creation of a sacred vessel that will be used by a spiritual being for a physical experience is what begins at conception? If so, when does that being actually become associated with that vessel? Is it at conception? Is it at birth? Is it somewhere in between?

To many people the questions above will seem ridiculous and pointless. For some they may stir a knowingness that lies deep within themselves. Others might feel anger or fear or guilt. Many religions seem to work overtime to ensure their congregants will feel those emotions enough when they do ask those kinds of questions they will think twice before asking them again.

So, what is the point? Can the answers to any of them be scientifically established one way or the other? Is there any value that might be gleaned from pondering such questions even if they cannot be so proven? Can the answers be known to some degree of confidence even if we are not able to scientifically verify them?

Marilou McIntryre made a powerful and succinct statement with her book title, *Life is Forever—Get Used To It*. I like the sentiment but I might express it a little more along the following line; "Life is forever—It would seem wise to make better plans for the rest of it than those we have made to the present".

Right now is an important part of our forever. It is where we are focused at the moment. Where we go from here is up to us. That does not mean we have to go it alone. We have established there is a spiritual aspect to the human condition. That would imply a powerful source of assistance available to us. But we are the ones who are going to have to make it work. It does not take a painstaking look around our world to realize we haven't calculated things out real carefully or it would not be in such turmoil. It is time for us to take a step back, figure out just how we have gotten ourselves into these jams, and then, equipped with greater understanding, begin to move forward with more prudence.

The Bible is an amazing book and there are great truths, both literal and metamorphic, that can be derived from its words. One concept the Bible does get literally right is when it boldly declares in several places "We are all God's children". We are all heirs of the Divine and, therefore, each of us possesses a portion of the Divine as a part of who we are. Alan Jackson captured the spirit of that Biblical Truth beautifully in the following lyrics of his song:

Here comes a Baptist, here comes a Jew
There goes a Mormon and a Muslim too
I see a Buddhist and a Hindu
I see a Catholic and I see you

We're all God's children
We're all God's children
We're all God's children
Why can't we be one big happy family?

But there are many in our world who would boldly claim there is no God. That idea is a delusion, a fantasy, a false hope born of ignorance, superstition, and fear they say. They would use sound logic to substantiate their claim. They would look around the world and note the hunger, misery and despair of so many millions and rationally and legitimately ask; "How could a God that loves us permit such things to be?"

The implied assumption in that question is if there was a God who loved us, He would intervene to relieve the burdens so many of us bear. But sound logic will not prove a proposition if the assumptions to which it is applied cannot bear the weight of truth. We have seen, for example, how classical evolution applies impeccable logic to build a magnificent idea that dead-ends in absurdity because at least one assumption to which that logic is applied cannot possibly be true.

And what about the assumption if there was a God who loved us, He would automatically intervene to relieve us from our misery and despair? In a universe of free will how could a God who loved us possibly be able to force that love upon us through that method of intervention? How successful has anyone ever been in trying to force their love upon another? Love cannot be given, even from God, if it is not both able and willing to be received.

Nonetheless, I do believe there is a God, Goddess, Allah, All That Is, whatever label you want to give it, that does love us and from Him/Her we have all received many things. These include an inherent freedom and the ability to discern and to make choice. I am also confident this gift set includes a "Forever" for us to use to learn to get it right. That would also mean we have just as long to keep on getting it wrong if that is what we insist upon. In fact I know some folks who just might succeed in doing that. But, if they do, it will be the result of a lot of stubborn choices and not a punishment from God.

Life in this world was never intended to be as harsh as it often is. But we have been given free will and, let's face it; we have managed to use that to create some rather serious problems for ourselves, both on an individual and a societal level. But there are solutions to our troubles and I believe there is an inexhaustible love and boundless wisdom available to help us uncover those solutions. We must learn, however, to allow that love to become a part of us. We have the means and capability to figure things out and begin to change, first ourselves, and then our world any time that is what we decide to do.

Before expanding upon the preceding speculations, I would like to take a moment to discuss another criticism I received on the book's earlier version. The exact statement was "Metaphysics cannot be used as a substitute for physics." This is the kind of oblique statement that seems to dominate so much communication taking place in our world today. Politicians have become masters at it with their so called "talking points". The statement is obviously true, so who would disagree with it? I suspect what this critic really thinks is that metaphysics should not be used at all in any spiritual or scientific discussion. But he didn't state that directly because doing so would likely not be well received by quite a few people. So, instead, he makes a meaningless true statement everybody can agree with and which will also produce a subtle influence to induce some toward his real and stronger point of view.

I will now try to make my position as clear as possible regarding the criticism. I completely agree with the statement. Obviously, metaphysics cannot be used as a substitute for physics. However, I would modify that statement by suggesting metaphysics can, and should, be used *in conjunction with* physics. In addition I would suggest it should be used in combination with every other science, every religion, and every other philosophy attempting to explore the mysteries of our existence.

The "classical" scientific fields, including chemistry, biology, physics, and astronomy, have performed wonders utilizing the scientific method to help us understand our world and universe. I do not know if I am more astonished at what I am learning when I watch a program like Nova on television or the imaginative ways in which I am learning it.

Science is also responsible for an array of gadgets and devices that have helped provide us with more comfortable, enhanced, and longer lives. But, unless it suits its purpose, if an idea cannot be observed, heard, or measured on a repeatable basis it is ignored by "classical" science. That is fine. Science has done a decent job defining the boundaries beyond which it will not go to explore those ideas it cannot directly observe and measure.

The problem is many "scientists" have taken this self-defined limitation "science" has put on itself and expanded it to include the idea if their "science" cannot fit a concept into its self-imposed boundaries for study, then it simply doesn't exist. They usually do not do this with so many words. No, like most successful propagandists they are far more subtle than that. But make no mistake about it, the scientific disciplines have become successful at convincing us if something is not "testable by their methods" then, by extension, it also cannot exist. As a result, "science" has become "God" for many people.

There is extensive subjective evidence to indicate mind can have a direct effect on matter without the use of neural systems. The nature of consciousness is such that I doubt it's going to sit still long enough for us to ever perform too many double-blind experiments on it. Thus, when attempting to understand its nature, we might have to rely on methods and reasoning the "scientist" may find distasteful. That, however, is not a reason to discard it.

Anecdotal evidence has often been enough by itself to send people out of this world. If we are going to do that, then surely we can give it some credence when attempting to understand how any of us came into it. There have been thousands of stories from every society in the world of events many might consider strange or impossible. Unexplained phenomena such as out of body experiences, lucid dreaming, channeling, near death experiences, apparitions, clairvoyance, and clairaudience all provide evidence at least certain aspects of the mind operate independently from the brain. The official position of the scientific establishment, and the unofficial position of many people, is to categorically dismiss such claims as over imagination. They then simply dispose them in a bin they call the "supernatural", and "That takes care of that."

But it is not reasonable to think they can get away so easily with calling *all* these people liars, crazy, gullible, or accuse them of being in a delusional state. Many such stories are compelling and well documented. I do not believe in the "supernatural" either. I don't even know what that would be. But I am convinced the incredible number of these stories calls for a closer look into the possibility they may suggest the "natural" extends into places we might want to consider checking out a little further even if traditional science is not currently equipped or willing to explore them.

A wife claims to see and talk to a material vision of a husband who has just passed away. A mother has a dream of her son in a car accident at the exact instant it really happens. Someone professes to be a medium and able to communicate with the "dead".

Science says, "Well those are extraordinary claims. Let me see you do it again." The wife never has another vision. The mother never has another dream anything like the one she reported. The medium, who may have been validated 100 straight times, describes someone who he claims to be communicating with on "the other side" that bears no resemblance to anyone known to the person he is talking to on "this side". So the "scientist" says "Well, that is a strange coincidence" or "it must be a lie" or "they ought to lock that person up for fraud". Clearly, not all scientists will take such cynical views of accounts such as these, but far too many do.

We should all be skeptical of unusual claims people make. I hope anybody who reads this book will do so with that mindset. But when the skepticism turns to cynicism, as it so often does when those claims involve the paranormal, it is time to give them a closer look. The sheer volume provides an enormous amount of anecdotal evidence there are many things that exist in our world and universe for which we have no ready answers. Many books have been written on this subject. I do not intend to reiterate those writings to any great detail in this one.

But I would like to discuss briefly two extraordinary people who have provided us much opportunity for further speculation. These are Edgar Cayce and Jane Roberts.

Edgar Cayce's story is one familiar to many Americans. He has often been referred to as America's psychic. He was born in Kentucky in 1877. He was raised in the Disciples of Christ church and was a devout Christian his entire life. He was 67 when he died in 1945 having read the entire Bible once for every year of his life. His compelling story is told in the book "*There is a River*" by Thomas Joseph Sugrue.

In 1898 Cayce developed a case of laryngitis and lost his voice for several weeks. He was hypnotized by a friend and, while in that state, prescribed a cure that worked to restore it. From that humble beginning he began a career that eventually led him to Virginia Beach, Virginia. There, in 1932, he established the Association for Research and Enlightenment (*ARE*).

Cayce originally became best known for his ability to go into a self-induced trance from which he would diagnose medical conditions for people and offer suggestions to cure them. He became famous across the country for his work because these recommendations almost always proved effective if followed according to his instructions.

In 1923 Cayce began doing a series of readings for the famous Theosophist, Arthur Lammers. In one session he included events from a past life in his diagnosis for the client. This reading almost induced Cayce to stop giving them altogether because reincarnation was a concept completely alien to the spiritual ideas he embraced. He became convinced, however, there was something to this concept. In the end he was able to incorporate that philosophy in to his fundamental Christian belief set. Past life experiences soon became a common part of the diagnoses and evaluations he would give to people.

At this time, many of Cayce's readings also began to include predictions for our planet's future. Some of these have proven true and others have not, including the slippage of California into the Pacific Ocean. At my last check that great state is still a part of the union.

Many people have used these failed predictions in an attempt to completely discredit all his work. Now, I do find it strange that in almost any other endeavor, perfection is not even expected. Michael Jordan may have made most of the shots he took at the basket, but he still missed quite a few. Even Jack Nicklaus put a drive into the woods now and then. But, for some reason, a onetime miss by a medium or psychic marks them forever more as a fraud in the minds of many people. The truth is Edgar Cayce was right a lot more than he was wrong. His overall body of work is extremely well documented and today the *ARE* is a highly respected organization in teaching and promoting the esoteric sciences.

Jane Roberts was a mystic and an author who lived in Elmira, New York. She became famous in the 1970's and 1980's for a series of books she co-authored with her husband, Robert Butts. These books documented channeled readings she gave for an entity known as Seth.

The following is an excerpt taken from the Seth Audio collection.

[1] "Your beliefs form reality. Your individual beliefs and your joint beliefs. Now the intensity of a belief is extremely important. And, if you believe, in very simple terms, that people mean you well, and will treat you kindly, they will. And, if you believe that the world is against you, then so it will be in your experience. And, if you believe . . . IF YOU BELIEVE THAT YOU WILL BEGIN TO DETERIORATE AT 22, then so you shall.

And, if you believe that you are poor, and always will be, then so your experience will so prove to you. Your beliefs meet you in the face when you look in the mirror. They form your image. You cannot escape your beliefs. They are, however, the method by which you create your experience.

It is important that you here realize that you are not at the mercy of the unexplainable, that you are not at the mercy of events over which you have no control whether those events are psychological events or physical ones, in your terms. As I have told you, there is little difference if you believe that your present life is caused by incidents in your early infancy or by past lives over which equally you feel you have no control. Your events, your lives, your experiences, are caused by your present beliefs. Change the beliefs and your life changes."—*Seth*

Following are quotes from a "Seth Book" called *Dreams, "Evolution, and Value Fulfillment Volume 1.*

² "While you believe that consciousness somehow emerges from dead matter, you will never understand yourselves, and you will always be looking for the point at which life took on form. You will always have to wonder about a kind of mechanical birth of the universe."

³ "Scientists now say that matter and energy are one. They must take the next full step to realize that consciousness and matter and energy are one."

⁴ "In certain terms, science and religion are both dealing with the idea of an objectively created universe. Either God "made it", or physical matter, in some unexplained manner, was formed after an initial explosion of energy, and consciousness emerged from that initially dead matter in a way yet to be explained. Instead consciousness *formed* matter. As I have said before, each atom and molecule has its own consciousness. Consciousness and matter and energy are one, but consciousness *initiates* the transformation of energy into matter."

Most of the buzz that has come from the camp of the quantum physicists over the last 20 years has swirled around something they have dubbed string theory. I would not pretend to have more than a rudimentary understanding of this concept. I do know, however, the idea that consciousness is something that came into existence in conjunction with the evolution of neural systems is absurd. I also know the notion that consciousness is something that can *only* be generated as a result of biological and chemical activity in the brain is absurd. There is a substantial amount of solid science surrounding both of these ideas. Much, in fact, points straight at both of them as being true. But it does not go all the way. A considerable leap of faith is required from where the science leaves off to the point where it is actually possible to embrace them as beliefs. Many people have made that leap, however, and a lot of those have made heavy emotional investments in that jump. When the combination of partial science, faith, and passion is used to hold together an unrealistic belief, it can be a tough nut to crack and I do not expect either idea to go down without a struggle. But, at some point, they will. When that happens, it would be good to have something more reasonable prepared to take over.

I think we already do have that replacement and it is all warmed up and ready to go. It centers on the main topic of speculation we have been discussing throughout the last several chapters. A careful examination of all the evidence compellingly points to the conclusion consciousness is a fundamental component of basic essence and some level of it is contained in everything.

When Brian Green attempts to convey his remarkable vision of what string theory is all about, I confess to getting more than a little mystified. I have noticed, however, those little squiggly lines he talks about sound suspiciously similar to what Seth was describing way back in 1971 in his discussion on what he called consciousness units, or CUs, in Jane Robert's book, *The Seth Material*. I have never heard Mr. Green offer an opinion as to whether he thought there was any level of consciousness in his strings, but I don't find it surprising there are others who have considered the possibility of a link between them and Seth's CUs. In fact, I suspect there are quite a few people who have perceived their conspicuous similarity.

One who has made that observation is best-selling author, David Wilcock. Mr. Wilcock has taken that connection to greater lengths than anybody else, however, in an extraordinary effort to establish sound scientific relationships between the strings of string theory and the CUs of Seth. In *The Seth Material*, Seth discusses a universe that rises out of [5]"cubes within cubes" and one made up of "a myriad of interconnecting wires, constantly trembling." As Mr Wilcock discusses in his book, *Shift of the Ages—Convergence Volume 1*, "this description from Seth is virtually identical to the fundamental ideas of string theory, which also discusses cubes within cubes as "hypercubes," and builds the universe on a matrix of interconnecting strings that vibrate".

For anyone interested in exploring this connection further I would recommend visiting Mr. Wilcock's website, *divinecosmos.com*. This site includes both the written and audio versions of Chapter 6 from his book *Shift of the Ages—Convergence Volume 1*. This chapter discusses in detail the startling comparisons between the ideas Seth brought forth over forty years ago and the latest discoveries in string theory.

Many ideas have originated within metaphysics that were later considered or verified by classical physics. The idea that consciousness is a fundamental component of matter and energy, however, was actually first proposed by conventional physicists over a half century before Seth brought it up in the early 1970's. I suspect the fact classical science later abandoned it was due more to prejudice than an honest examination of the evidence. Neils Bohr, David Bohm, Max Plank, and Wolfgang Pauli, among others, argued with great conviction and lucidity there were strange things going on at the quantum levels that defied rational explanations. To Albert Einstein, however, it was simply unacceptable to think there might be universal aspects that could not be logically and reliably described and predicted. Mr. Einstein had a well-deserved reputation for solid thinking. It was primarily due to his persuasion the idea that consciousness was something existing at the basic levels of matter and energy has lain dormant for the last seventy years.

The notion that an atom might have some level of consciousness is apparently too fantastic for most modern scientists to even consider. Up to now they have been fairly successful at shoving it into the background of classical scientific footnotes. But it is beginning to force its way back into recognition as a possible means to explain concepts we have been unable to do any other way. I think there is good reason to believe it is the phoenix of physics and it will be rising soon.

Ten

Religion, Politics, and Science

Never discuss religion or politics, as the saying goes, if you want to keep the peace. But there are currently 400 wars and guerrilla actions going on around the world. There are fifty million Americans, including thirty million children, living below the poverty line. Approximately five billion people subsist on the equivalent of $10 a day or less and almost half on $2.50. Should we be surprised there is such turmoil in our world? I do not think so.

Religion and politics have enormous influence in how we construct our societies. They have both failed us in many ways and that old adage is clearly wrong. If we want to have any chance to create the peace and transform our world they need to be discussed. That exchange demands we do it openly, rationally, and in the context of their relationship with respect to each other.

Freedom of religion is an important and valuable part of our national heritage. The relationship anyone develops with the divine is going to be personal and unique. That connection will also be based on conclusions reached in ways other than through logic and reason. A total understanding of our spirituality is far beyond anyone's comprehension.

For these reasons I would not question or care about anyone's religious beliefs whatever those might happen to be. Until, that is, they begin to promote those beliefs as a reason for influencing actions that affect the general public.

One of our country's treasures is that everyone can have a voice in determining how it is going to function. It is inevitable that voice will, from time to time, be influenced by religious beliefs. There is nothing inherently wrong with that. But, when it does happen, it also means those beliefs are voluntarily being made available for objective evaluation by everybody. What is wrong is an effort to thwart that appraisal by misusing the freedom afforded by the constitution. How often have we heard religious groups claim a public policy interferes with their right to practice their beliefs without also being willing to participate in an impartial assessment of those beliefs?

We all have an obligation to try and verify to the greatest degree possible any conviction used in an effort to influence public policy reaches an acceptable standard of plausibility. Today the political process has essentially been brought to a halt. There are a variety reasons for that unhappy fact, but religious dogma is at the heart of far too many of them.

In my view, the concept a loving God would condemn any of His creatures to eternal torment does not rise to any acceptable level of plausibility no matter what reason might be suggested to justify it. There are obviously many who would heatedly disagree with that opinion. But I think the majority, including a large number who hear the idea repeated every Sunday, would agree it really does not make much sense.

The literal idea that Jesus died on the cross to make it possible for us to get to heaven is also mutually exclusive with the theory of reincarnation. They cannot both be factually true. But *God Theories* scientifically proves reincarnation is a reasonable option. That means it, does, therefore, rise to an acceptable level of plausibility. That, coupled with evidence from many other sources, strongly suggest it is a part of the way in which our reality functions.

Religious beliefs, however, can have both literal and metaphorical interpretations. The idea Jesus died on the cross so we can get to heaven and the philosophy of reincarnation, for example, might be mutually exclusive on a literal level. But I think there is much truth that lies beneath the surface that can be found in each. In other words I do believe there are valid reasons to support the passion displayed by many who would call themselves Christians. There is certainly much wisdom that can be gleaned from the words of Jesus as they are reported in the Bible. I have no hard evidence to support it, but I also happen to believe he is real and able in some mysterious way to be a source of love, joy, and strength to those open, able, and willing to receive those energies from him.

Now some might argue if that is true, then why worry about it? If there is justification for that passion, what difference does it make the exact ideas put forth in conjunction with it? I would contend it makes a huge difference simply because words matter. Words convey ideas and ideas generate emotions. If the words produce false ideas then the generated emotions will be faulty and we will continue to have such things as crusades, inquisitions, witch hunts, and their modern day equivalent of congress people refusing to talk to each other and the resulting national and world crises that condition engenders and perpetuates.

If a belief is maintained solely through a combination of blind faith and passion, then there is no room left for reason. That also means there is no room left for discussion. That might not be a problem if the belief is about an issue that does not affect other people or if there are no other people who hold a differing view. But all too often that is not the case. So what should be a thoughtful discussion instead turns into a shouting match and one that too frequently spills into the streets. Probably the first controversy that picture brings to mind in this country is the one surrounding the subject of abortion.

What I find most interesting about this issue is that virtually everybody who has an emotional feeling about it agrees on almost everything about it. The members of any Pro-Life group and those of Planned Parenthood all have the same ultimate goal to create a world free of abortion. Virtually everybody is pro-life whether we favor legalized abortion or not. Everyone believes in the sanctity of life whether they believe in God or not. We all desire to leave a world to our children and grand-children in which they will be able to dream and fulfill those dreams.

The unfortunate adoption of the labels pro-life and pro-choice to mark those with differing views around the legal issue of abortion has done much to perpetuate the myth one group holds life more precious than the other. One important action we could easily take that would lead to a more reasonable approach to assessing the merits concerning this subject would be to simply dispense with those characterizations.

All groups that profess differing views on the controversy agree abortion, at some point, needs to become a thing of the past. About the only thing they disagree on is when that should happen. Some people think it should be now. Others say now is not the time. There are valid reasons to support both views. But we need to bring the exchanges around this issue off from the streets and down from the billboards. We need to move the conversation to venues that would enable it to become the more reasoned deliberation it deserves to be.

The potential of what our world could someday become may be unlimited, but it is made up of only so much area and volume. It contains only so many barrels of oil. It can withstand only so much physical and emotional abuse. It can support and sustain only so much life as we know it and desire it to be. There are many reasons for the various challenges we face today. Most, in one way or another, revolve around energy and material resource availability and the methods we use to distribute those resources to the seven billion people who currently occupy the planet.

Is the world already overpopulated? Many would say yes and many no. Personally I believe it could indefinitely sustain our current population *if* we all got along. We could then devote time and energy to solving our basic problems. We could find alternative resources instead of using so many we have to destroy what remains of that supply. But we don't all get along and, until we start doing that better, it is imperative we do more to limit the expansion of the human population.

Obviously, the best method of population control is to choose those actions and precautions required to prevent conception in the first place. But we seem to have provided neither the moral ground upon which to stand nor adequate instruction to our younger generations as they move into adulthood as to just what that entails. There are nearly 750,000 teen pregnancies in our country every year. One of three girls will have a child while still a teen and nearly 80% will be unmarried. It is the highest such rate in the industrialized world.

The average woman in Afghanistan is a mother seven times before the age of thirty. By the time her children are eight years old, one will be dead. Some will be working eight hours a day in a shoe factory. Others will already be in the process of being seduced by the Taliban or Al Qaida. Before the youngest reaches fifteen, their mother will be dead. These are themes repeated in far too many places across our globe.

We, the people of this planet, have made the collective choice to bring a massive number of children into our world for whom the love and resources which they deserve does not exist. This has not been either a wise or a responsible choice and we are experiencing the consequences we should expect from having made it.

There is overwhelming evidence to suggest slower population growth and investing in reproductive health, women's empowerment, and education reduce poverty. It should be obvious to everyone we simply cannot expect to sustain our world as a place to live if we bring as many people in to it as we are physically able to do. Yet that appears the position several religious groups uphold as they fight even the efforts by the government to require health insurance companies to cover the cost of contraceptives. Fortunately that position does appear the minority. But the religious opposition being generated is still making it more difficult than it should be to enact this common sense requirement.

A fetus is not part of a woman's body she should feel free to eliminate for that reason. It is a developing vehicle intended for use by a spiritual being and is, therefore, sacred. As we have demonstrated, however, the fetus cannot be the ultimate source for that being's existence. It is a fair question to consider whether there might be far more opportune times for such a being to be born into this world than the ones that often present themselves. Given the current stress we are placing on the planet, if a prospective Mother in concurrence with those whom she seeks counsel comes to the decision to have an abortion, I believe it should be allowed to proceed and without the interference that is so commonly associated with that action.

The related issues of abortion, contraception, and population control are the ones generating the most emotion among religious groups. But the attempts to bring God into the classroom are not far behind. There has been a strong push in recent years by some to force the public schools to teach a version of creationism wherever evolution is also taught. In 1981, an Arkansas law was passed mandating equal time for teaching creation science and evolution. This law was declared unconstitutional. A similar act was passed in Louisiana, which was also deemed unconstitutional by the Supreme Court. In 1999, the Kansas School Board declared that students would no longer be tested on the theory of evolution with the intent to eliminate it from the curriculum. The school board was voted out from office, and the law was overturned. In June, 2008, Louisiana passed a bill allowing teachers of evolution to present evidence both for and against the theory. Various groups have opposed this law and see it as an attempt to incorporate the teaching of religion into the public schools. The law specifically forbids promoting any particular religion.

We can be confident the effort to force an alternative to balance the teaching of classical evolution in the public schools by the proponents of creationism and intelligent design will continue. At some point, they may be successful. That possibility should concern us all. Not because their ideas are loony tunes off-the-wall craziness. They are not that. But, if they were to get their own course, it would effectively stifle many voices that should be heard in such a discussion. That would be a tragedy.

The founders of our country were wise men. Many were Masons. This organization incorporates but one of the numerous sets of thoughts attempting to explain aspects of the unexplainable. But these men also realized the need to seek a closer working relationship with God was an individual matter and they insisted on creating a society where this was possible. At the same time, they recognized the need for the separation of church and state and made this concept a legal and generally accepted part of our government. This separation is a difficult one to define and can easily be crossed without our even being aware it has happened. But there are times it is clear we have done so.

One of these is the creation of the political yardstick as to how devout a Christian someone has to be in order to even consider running for president. Taxpayer dollars used for faith-based charities is another example. Others are the full-page advertisements we see in national newspapers placed by religious organizations encouraging people not to vote for various candidates because of their views on certain social issues. Yet, all these groups have retained their tax-exempt status. Many other religious groups have passed out flyers with candidates voting records on issues of their particular concern. Others have become active in passing laws such as Proposition 8 in California and they, too, have retained their tax-exempt status.

All religions, both by definition and precedence, function primarily in the domain beyond logic and reason. From here they have explored many mysteries of our universe. Each has brought back into our everyday world ideas and techniques that have enabled us to gain a greater sense of the loving Creator I believe exists at the heart of that universe. From these endeavors each has also accumulated its own rich and beautiful traditions. These have helped many to communicate with and develop their personal relationship with that Creator.

But, in addition to all the beautiful things religion has given us, every one has also brought back dark and otherwise questionable ideas that have, from time to time, taken hold in our world. These have had, and continue to have, terrible repercussions on humanity and the planet. The appearance may be different than it was four hundred years ago, but religious intolerance, discrimination, and zealotry are still alive in all parts of the world.

It would not be fair to expect ideas, thoughts, and beliefs that have been discovered or engendered through journeys beyond logic and reason to be either provable or disprovable by the methods of logic and reason. However, there are exceptions to that expectation. These will undoubtedly increase in number as we gain in understanding.

Science and religion have historically been seen as irreconcilable antagonists. This perception is well deserved. Unfortunately, the actions that have helped formulate that assessment continue happening all too often today. But what both science and religion need to learn is that the other functions in a legitimate domain of consciousness. And they need to do it sooner rather than later. The world is not in a position to put up with their squabbling much longer. We have serious issues that need immediate attention and these can be dealt with much more easily without that distraction.

There is at least one vital lesson for each to assimilate before they are likely to call a halt to their bickering. Science needs to recognize there are questions for which reasonable answers will almost certainly never be found. They can continue to bang their heads against the wall trying to figure out such things as why there is something instead of nothing if they want. But, on occasion, they need to pause and take a moment to bask in the glow and wonder of mystery. And they need to do it for no other reason than simply because "It's a mystery. Maybe nobody will ever know".

The essential concept all religions need to learn is that the phrase "within reason" applies to them as much as it does to everybody else. "Because I said so"; "Just have faith"; "Because it's written in this book"; are not going to be acceptable answers forever, even for establishing religious beliefs. Within reason, even "blind" faith can be a beautiful part of many things, but using it as an excuse to essentially "believe" anything is not appropriate.

The spat between science and religion is not the sole cause of our many problems. But on the day science embraces mystery and religion acknowledges and begins to act upon its accountability to reason, the world will stop and turn around. It will begin to climb out from the muck of chaos, anger, misery, hunger, despair, and domination that comprise so much of it today to become the one filled with joy, happiness, contentment, dominion, and love it was always meant to be.

"Fat chance of that" says the cynic. Well, even in his sarcasm he is correct. It won't happen by chance of any kind, fat or otherwise. It will happen by the collective and individual design of people with vision from every corner of the globe. We cannot say how long it's going to take and there won't be any dates to circle on the calendar to mark the progress. There will always be room for the cynic if he insists on staying where he is. Eventually, though, there won't be much for him to do and he might start to get a little lonely. I suspect at some point he, too, will come along.

I would ordinarily be opposed to teaching esoteric or religious theories on the origin of life in the public schools because it is, essentially, a personal issue. However, there are three driving factors which are encouraging me to change that view. The first is the pressing need for science and religion to recognize their legitimate roles are to complement each other rather than to act as adversaries. The second is the increased tendency we are seeing from religious groups to become involved in public policy. The third is the fact the intelligent designers do have a valid point in their opposition to many ideas put forth by classical evolution and in their feelings these should be balanced by offering different perspectives.

All these concerns do need to be addressed. Introducing a course into the public schools that would seek to objectively discuss the various points of view revolving around the "God" question has the potential to go a long way towards meeting that need.

My major concern with allowing the intelligent design activists to begin offering classes on their views is it would pit one advocacy group in direct opposition to another. If we ever do allow public school curricula to include discussions on esoteric theory, it must be far more inclusive and taught under strict guidelines.

Because of the strong emotions that are frequently generated in conjunction with these beliefs, we need to tread carefully here. The input from many people would need to be involved in the detail planning. The overriding intention such a course should have would be the objective dissemination of information. There would need to be a clear statement it is *not* to be an advocacy for any final belief set. It must include input from several religions, atheist and humanist organizations, the metaphysical sciences, and other pertinent groups. We are a long way from implementing such a course, but I believe there is merit in its careful consideration as a possible future course of action.

The next great socio revolution that is going to occur in our world will come in the area of artificial intelligence. The Singularity, as it has come to be called, carries with it both unbound potential as well as significant risks. The essential component of this broad based idea is that advances in computer and nanotechnology will, in the near future, make human beings and machines essentially indistinguishable. Much of the futuristic envisioning entailed in this idea is put forth by American author and inventor, Raymond Kurzweil.

Mr. Kurzweil in his 2005 book *The Singularity is Near* predicts that by 2045 [1]"$1000 will buy a computer a billion times more intelligent than every human combined. This means that average and even low-end computers will be vastly smarter than even highly intelligent, unenhanced humans. This technological singularity occurs as artificial intelligences (AIs) surpass human beings as the smartest and most capable life forms on the Earth. Technological development is taken over by the machines which can think, act and communicate so quickly that normal humans cannot even comprehend what is going on. The machines enter into a "runaway reaction" of self-improvement cycles with each new generation of AIs appearing faster and faster. From this point onwards, technological advancement is explosive, under the control of the machines, and thus cannot be accurately predicted (hence the term "Singularity")."

What Mr. Kurzweil is predicting regarding the phenomenal breakthroughs in artificial intelligence and medical technology does appear to be the direction we are heading. But at least one aspect of his vision suggests a major error in judgment. He seems to think dying is a bad idea. Now, I am all for postponing that action until one is ready to do it. That state would obviously be influenced by any number of factors and I have no problem with extending this current life for 50, 100, 200 or more years to help us more effectively reach that point. But, in spite of his protestations to the contrary, the time will come when each of us will be ready to move on to grander and greater things than even he envisions.

But will humans transcend biology as he suggests? Yes, I believe they will and that technology will play a significant role in facilitating that phenomenon. In fact it is already beginning to do that with advances in such things as stem cell research and unraveling the human genetic code. But we also know everyone transcends biology the moment they die without the need for any technology (At least of the human variety). The Singularity has enormous potential to help us prepare for that transition more gracefully. But it is also vital to ensure as we move towards it we do not succeed in creating Frankenstein's monster after all.

There is much we will never know about our remarkable universe, but we can no longer reasonably doubt that a spiritual component is an integral part of it. In this book we have focused on using science to help come to that conclusion. But there are millions around the world who would readily affirm science is not needed for the job. They would identify with the words of Johnny Cash in his song "My God is real for I can feel Him in my soul". There is a part inside each of us that knows the Truth in those words. There are too many, however, who have sealed off that knowingness and nailed it shut with anger, blame, bigotry, self-doubt, fear, despair, greed, hate, lethargy, martyrdom, prejudice, and a need for domination and control.

Fear does have its rightful place, but it can also be a seductive place for us to hide. Discrimination extends far beyond the color of our skin and we would be lying if we said we've never done it. And is there any among us who can say we have never placed blame where it had no right to be?

We are spiritual beings, but right now we are also human beings. We are in this world to enjoy it and learn some things. One of the most important of those is to come to understand the difference between struggle and challenge. None of us will ever glide with perfect grace over the obstacles we place, or allow to be placed, in our lives. But neither were we ever meant to get mired so deeply in our daily battles we lose touch with the magnificent beings we truly are.

Contrary to what many people have concluded, our universe does have a purpose. That is to provide the opportunity for eternal and unlimited potential of expression. Our purpose is to learn how to take advantage of that opportunity by creating, co-creating, and manifesting the expressions of our choice. We will get better at it. Ultimately our goal is to learn how to make them fun, enjoyable, and exciting. We are here to learn how to love and how to receive love. Certainly we each have our own individual and unique reasons for coming into this world at this time. But the purposes for everything we will ever do, and the motives for traveling to wherever it is we will ever go, will always involve those fundamentals. They are at the heart of our ever expanding and never ending journey of returning home to God, to Goddess, to All That Is, to the ultimate Source of our very being.

Forty years ago I would have considered myself to be an agnostic. I thought the "God" question was one that could never be proven one way or the other and I was pretty much ready to let it go at that. My conversion from that belief was a conscious one. I came to realize, in my mind at least, our world simply could not be the way it is without some kind of outside deliberated intervention. Once I came to that realization, I knew there was nothing more important I could ever do than learn all I could about the Incredible Intelligence that must be behind that deliberation. An open minded exploration of that concept from virtually every conceivable point of view has been my passion ever since.

My own conversion from agnosticism to a confirmed belief in a divine presence initially involved the logical mind. But any such relationship must eventually become experiential to make it real. There are probably as many ways to do that as there are people who have ever lived. Some may do it through meditation or prayer. A walk in the woods, tending a garden, a round of golf, church on a Sunday morning, or a cold beer in a smoky bar room on Saturday night might be the way for others. These days we might have to settle for one without the smoke, but, however we do it, on occasion we need to find a way to push in the clutch and coast awhile and give our souls a chance to catch up to us.

I have expressed many personal beliefs in this book and I have also raised several controversial issues. It is safe to say both come with the territory. But if trying to tell people what to think or inflaming passions had been the motives for writing it, the first word would never have been put to paper.

Our planet is in trouble. I believe the most underlying reason is because too many of us have lost a sense of connection with our spirituality. If that is true, the most important thing we can do to heal our world is make sure enough of us get reconnected. But I have said my piece on that. If there is one single statement that could be made with absolute certainty, it would be that none of us have all the right answers and some of the answers all of us have are wrong. So it is time now for me to listen to what it is you have to say. Because even amidst the chaos, there are subtle indications we are on the verge of transforming our world into the oasis it was always meant to be. But that won't happen by chance or fate either. It's a job that's going to take the both of us.

References

Chapter Four

1. The Observer (25, January 1931)
2. Wikipedia—The Free Encyclopedia, Science Portal, Uncertainty Principle Web Page

Chapter Nine

1. The Seth Audio Collection, Vol 1, Tape 1
2. Dreams, "Evolution, and Value Fulfillment Volume 1" A Seth Book, p108; Jane Roberts
3. Dreams, "Evolution, and Value Fulfillment Volume 1" A Seth Book, p108; Jane Roberts
4. Dreams, "Evolution, and Value Fulfillment Volume 1" A Seth Book, p114; Jane Roberts
5. Divine Cosmos Web Page—Chapter six: The Seth Entity and Consciousness Units

Chapter Ten

1. Wikipedia, the free encyclopedia—Predictions Made by Ray Kurzweil

Index